THE
BIRMINGHAM TO
GLOUCESTER
LINE

THE
BIRMINGHAM TO GLOUCESTER LINE

COLIN G. MAGGS

AMBERLEY

Acknowledgements

The author wishes to express his gratitude for help given by W. F. Grainger, P. D. Nicholson, C. F. Roberts and D. R. Steggles.

Front cover: At Gloucester Eastgate, 18 April 1963, Class 5 4-6-0 No. 45263 heads the 16.15 Gloucester to Bristol. (*Author*)

Back cover: 'Patriot' Class 6 4-6-0 No. 45504 *Royal Signals* (82E, Bristol, Barrow Road) at Gloucester, 9 September 1960, comes off the Newcastle to Bristol express headed by 'Jubilee' Class 6 4-6-0 No. 45685 *Barfleur*. (*R. E. Toop*)

First edition 1986 (Line One Publishing Limited)
Enlarged second edition 2013

Amberley Publishing
The Hill, Stroud
Gloucestershire, GL5 4EP

www.amberley-books.com

Copyright © Colin G. Maggs, 2013

The right of Colin G. Maggs to be identified as the Author
of this work has been asserted in accordance with the
Copyrights, Designs and Patents Act 1988.

British Library Cataloguing in Publication Data.
A catalogue record for this book is available from the British Library.

ISBN 978 1 4456 0699 6

Typeset in 10pt on 12pt Sabon.
Typesetting and Origination by Amberley Publishing.
Printed in the UK.

Contents

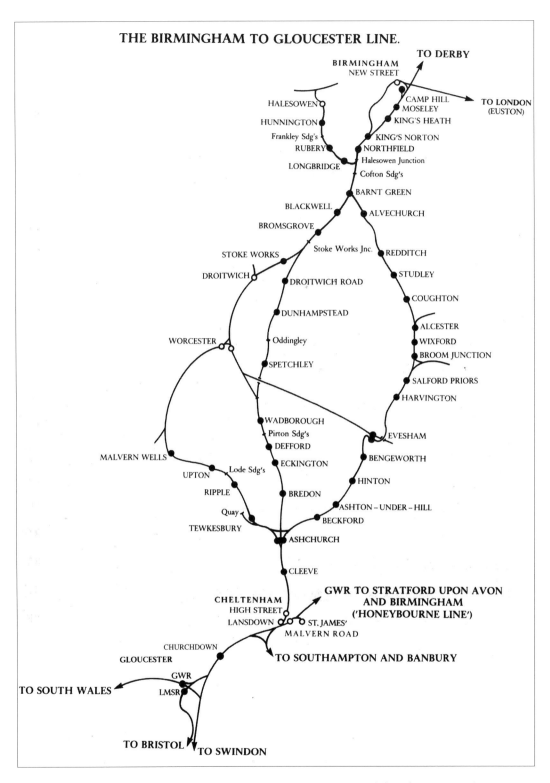

THE BIRMINGHAM TO GLOUCESTER LINE.

TO DERBY

BIRMINGHAM
NEW STREET

CAMP HILL
MOSELEY

TO LONDON
(EUSTON)

HALESOWEN

HUNNINGTON

Frankley Sdg's

RUBERY

LONGBRIDGE

KING'S HEATH

KING'S NORTON

NORTHFIELD

Halesowen Junction

Cofton Sdg's

BARNT GREEN

BLACKWELL

ALVECHURCH

BROMSGROVE

Stoke Works Jnc.

REDDITCH

STOKE WORKS

DROITWICH

DROITWICH ROAD

STUDLEY

COUGHTON

DUNHAMPSTEAD

ALCESTER

WORCESTER

Oddingley

WIXFORD

BROOM JUNCTION

SPETCHLEY

SALFORD PRIORS

HARVINGTON

WADBOROUGH

Pirton Sdg's

DEFFORD

EVESHAM

MALVERN WELLS

ECKINGTON

BENGEWORTH

UPTON

Lode Sdg's

RIPPLE

BREDON

HINTON

Quay

ASHTON – UNDER – HILL

TEWKESBURY

BECKFORD

ASHCHURCH

CLEEVE

CHELTENHAM
HIGH STREET

GWR TO STRATFORD UPON AVON
AND BIRMINGHAM
('HONEYBOURNE LINE')

LANSDOWN

ST. JAMES'
MALVERN ROAD

CHURCHDOWN

TO SOUTHAMPTON AND BANBURY

GLOUCESTER

GWR

TO SOUTH WALES

LMSR

TO BRISTOL

TO SWINDON

Note: To avoid confusion, the initials BGR are only used for the Birmingham &
Gloucester Railway, the Bristol & Gloucester Railway being written in full.

Train times follow the form given in the public timetables; therefore photographs
up to 16 June 1963 are given in the twelve-hour clock, i.e. 1.05 p.m., and after
June 1963 they are given in the twenty-four hour clock, i.e. 13.05.

Chapter One

The History of the Birmingham & Gloucester Railway

As early as 13 December 1824, a well-supported meeting was held in the White Lion Inn, Bristol, with the object of building a single-line railway to Birmingham via Gloucester, Tewkesbury and Worcester. The Bristol, Northern & Western Railway (BNWR) would have provided a useful link between the manufacturing area of Birmingham and the sea, capturing the brick and clay traffic of Stourbridge, salt from Droitwich and the products of the woollen mills of the Stroud valley. It would have given a rail outlet to the coal and paving stone from Coalpit Heath. There was certainly a need for a railway, as water transport to Bristol from Birmingham took six and a half days and the charge was £ 1 5s 0d a ton. Road transport was quicker, only taking three days, but the charge was £5. About 78,000 tons of goods were conveyed by water annually from Birmingham to Bristol and 5,000 tons by road, and there was also considerable reverse traffic.

The £50 BNWR shares were allocated thus: 16,000 to Bristol, 3,000 to landowners, 2,500 to Birmingham, 1,500 to Worcester, 1,000 to Gloucester and 1,000 to Ireland, the total amounting to £1.25 million. When the subscription list opened, 'a complete scramble took place, in which much ink was upset and pens spoilt in the eagerness of all to subscribe, and before the meeting broke up, the whole number of shares allotted to Bristol were taken up.' On 28 January 1825, the BNWR appointed Josias Jessop to the post of resident engineer (Jessop was chiefly remembered for his work as engineer to the Cromford & High Peak Railway). By June, W. H. Townsend, a Bristol surveyor and valuer who would later draft the Bristol end of the Great Western Railway, had planned the line from Gloucester almost to Worcester, but discovered that a line onwards to Birmingham would be difficult, as awkward topography made it impossible to avoid inclined planes, heavy cuttings and embankments.

On 15 June, it was agreed that the line would be built from Bristol to Worcester and that the portion onwards to Birmingham would be deferred. However, the financial crisis of 1826 caused a large number of subscribers to call for a complete abandonment of the project and a return of the deposit money, this course being agreed on 19 May. It was remarkable that as much as 17s 6d in the pound was returned to subscribers, only 2s 6d being kept to cover administrative costs and legal expenses.

In 1832, two members of the Society of Friends, Joseph and Charles Sturge, were employed by Brunel, then aged twenty-six, to survey an inexpensive line

The exterior of Cheltenham station, *c.* 1850. (*Author's collection*)

Cheltenham, view Down, *c.* 1850, showing the train shed. (*Author's collection*)

The Royal train at Cheltenham, 29 September 1849. (*Author's collection*)

between Birmingham and Gloucester. The project foundered through lack of funds and Brunel was captured by the Great Western Railway in March 1833.

In 1836 Captain William Scarth Moorsom was appointed to survey a line from Birmingham to Gloucester, being engaged on the terms of 'no success – no pay'. Moorsom, born in 1804 near Whitby, was educated at Sandhurst, where he learned surveying, and was the brother of Admiral Moorsom, who spent a brief time as chairman of the London & North Western Railway. Captain Moorsom engaged two ex-soldiers as his residential engineers, one for the Birmingham and the other for the Gloucester division. The Birmingham & Gloucester Railway engineering offices were conveniently situated in Foregate Street, Worcester, midway between the two termini. This building was later demolished to make room for the line to Malvern.

Although the best route from Birmingham to Gloucester would have been through Droitwich, Worcester and Tewkesbury, all these places were avoided because of the expense of extra mileage and the high cost of land near towns. Cheltenham, too, was planned to be missed, but such an uproar was created that the line was diverted there, the railway capturing the northern traffic from Cheltenham, which had a large mobile population seeking treatment and entertainment. The anticipated income received from Cheltenham could be set against the additional cost of £200,000 compared with only £750,000 for a direct line from Birmingham to Gloucester. One serious disadvantage of the new route was that it negotiated the Lickey Incline. To avoid this obstruction, Brunel had proposed carrying the line further east, which would have eased the gradient from 1 in 37.5 to a modest 1 in 300, but such a course would have skirted the towns by an even greater mileage and was thus rejected.

As some shareholders objected to the Lickey Incline, it was decided to consult Joseph Locke, engineer to the Grand Junction Railway running from Birmingham to Warrington. He reported that using the incline would be safer than travelling by coach on a turnpike road and he saw no justification to seek an alternative route. This statement resulted in the meeting expressing its confidence in Moorsom. Incidentally, one of Moorsom's assistants in the BGR engineering office at Worcester was the young Herbert Spencer, later to become a famous philosopher. Spencer's autobiography gives us an insight into Moorsom. In the spring of 1840 he wrote in his diary:

> Yesterday was spent in an excursion on the line. I started from this [meeting] with the Captain in his gig at 9 a.m., and accompanied him to Bromsgrove, where after spending an hour or so in examining the works, and getting some refreshment, we parted – he proceeding onward to Birmingham and I occupying the remainder of the day in walking back along the line.
>
> These, you see, are pretty good proofs that the Captain has not fallen off in his kind treatment ... He is, in fact, the best specimen of a perfect gentleman that I have ever come near. Mrs Moorsom, also, is quite as worthy of admiration in her conduct to all around her. I spent the whole of Good Friday with them, and taking the average since I have been here, I pass about two evenings in the week at their house.

Hours at the BGR Worcester office were 9.00 a.m. to 5.00 p.m., with an hour for lunch and Saturday afternoons free – very generous for the time. According to Spencer, many of the sub-assistants were the younger sons of gentry. Moorsom ran a club for his assistants where technical papers were presented, thus widening their minds. On a salary of £120 per annum, he received a rise of £15 in August 1839. Spencer was critical of his superiors, in one instance claiming that the method of track laying gave insufficient lateral support. This, he claimed, would lead to bulging due to the lateral oscillation of the locomotives. Events proved him correct.

In August 1840, Spencer was appointed Moorsom's technical secretary and learnt surveying and geology. In July 1840, he designed and superintended the construction of a replacement bridge at Bromsgrove. He was also responsible for the reconstruction of part of Avon Bridge, Defford, which proved weak and where a wing wall had failed. This required rebuilding without line closure, so one road was shut and trains ran on the other. He needed to excavate so much of the embankment that the running line had to be shored up. Work completed, his post on the BGR was terminated on 25 April 1841 and he was offered the job as assistant to the locomotive engineer, but turned it down to become a philosopher instead.

For level crossings between Cheltenham and Bromsgrove, Moorsom designed single-storey gate lodges, with octagonal, bay-fronted sections at one, or both, ends of the building and groups of narrow, round-headed window openings. He later reused these designs when responsible for the Southampton & Dorchester Railway. When the crossing keeper had a family, the MR built an upper storey.

The *Gloucester Journal* for 6 September 1836 was excited at the railway's potential:

When the merchant of Gloucester can go to that great emporium of manufactures, Birmingham, to breakfast, spend the day in the transaction of business, and return again the same evening; and when the manufacturer of merchant of Birmingham shall find the ships that are to carry his products to the most distant lands brought within two hours' ride of his own door; who can say to what an extent the commercial intercourse between these two places may be carried, and who can tell to what a pitch of importance our port and city may be raised by the completion of this great undertaking.

The first general meeting of the BGR was held on 19 September 1836 at Dee's Royal Hotel, Birmingham. The directors under the Act were Samuel Baker, Robert Canning, William Scale Evans, John Francis, William Fox, John Greene, Richard Hayward, Samuel Haines, John Kemp, Daniel Ledsam, Francis Lloyd, William Montague, Edward Tilsley Moore, James Pearson, Charles Sturge, James Maurice Shipton, Joseph Walker and William Wasborn. The Board of Management was divided into two committees: the Gloucester, which dealt with the line from Gloucester to Worcester, and the Birmingham, which oversaw Worcester to Birmingham. Each was independent of the other. Company meetings were held at Birmingham and Gloucester on an alternating basis. £1,000 was voted to the eighteen directors for their services, commencing 1 September.

They stated that they had managed to present the bill immediately on the opening of that Session of Parliament and it had secured a rapid progress through the various stages, being the first railway Act to receive Royal Assent that session. Lord Granville Somerset steered the bill through the Commons and the Marquis of Salisbury guided it through the Lords. The BGR Act, 6 & 7 William IV cap 14 of 22 April 1836, was supplemented by a further Act, 7 William IV cap 26 of 5 May 1837, for the construction of extensions to Worcester and Tewkesbury.

The directors reported that 'only one tunnel was planned, while gradients were easy, only in one place exceeding 1 in 300'. This statement craftily glossed over the exception, which was the Lickey Incline and intended that this be divided into two sections to facilitate working, remarking that it 'may occasion a delay of about five minutes as compared with other parts of the line. The planes will be worked by two stationary engines at less expense per mile than the locomotive portion of the line.' An agreement had been made with Captain Moorsom to retain the office of Engineer-in-Chief, he undertaking not to superintend more than one other railway in the same vicinity. His made his headquarters at No. 5 Hatherley Place, Cheltenham.

The first half-yearly report, presented on 1 February 1837, sounded a note of optimism. Engineering works had begun and capital was being subscribed 'with a commendable alacrity which left no doubt of the whole being obtained at the various periods at which it might be required'. However, this optimism was to prove short-lived. The following year proved brighter; good progress was made with the works and the geological formation had been found favourable.

In June 1837, the directors were told that construction could not begin, as some landowners were demanding too high a price for their property, causing the railway to take legal proceedings. In one case, £3,027 was demanded by the

BIRMINGHAM & GLOUCESTER

RAILWAY.

Report of Third Half-yearly General Meeting,

AUGUST 8th, 1837.

Title page of the report of the half-yearly meeting of the BGR, held on 8 August 1837.

owner, the BGR offered £650 and the jury awarded £752 11s 0d; while in another example the respective figures were £2,983, £600 and £852 11s 0d. In yet another example, the landowner claimed £12,000 but was awarded only £1,600.

The first contract was to be from Camp Hill, Birmingham, to Moseley, and the second from Moseley to Bredon Cross, but in August 1837 the directors agreed not to start work until almost the full amount of the unpaid calls was received, the period being one of 'unexampled monetary difficulty'. Some shareholders were worried about the capabilities of Captain Moorsom and approached Joseph Locke, engineer of the Grand Junction Railway, to check Moorsom's figures. Locke, reporting in September 1837, approved of Moorsom's plans.

On 31 October 1837, the directors advertised the contracts, and by the New Year work had started. In August 1838, they reported that all land, approximately 500 acres, had been purchased both for the main line and the Tewkesbury branch and that contractors were at work, but on 24 January 1839 a special meeting of shareholders was called to consider the very depressed state reached by the shares, this being caused by several directors having disposed of a large proportion of their holdings. News the following month was more encouraging. Two million of the 3.6 million cubic yards of earthworks had been excavated, a third of the brickwork and masonry was completed and some permanent way laid. It was anticipated that the cost of the main line and the Worcester branch would not exceed the capital of £950,000, this result only being achieved by adopting the plan of dividing the line into small contracts. It was decided that there would be no gain in opening the line from Cheltenham to Droitwich as, through lack of a coaching establishment there, passengers would have been unable to travel on to Birmingham. Instead, it was intended to press on to Bromsgrove, where coaching facilities were provided.

Even before the line was complete, thought had been given to the working of traffic up the Lickey Incline. Both Brunel and Stephenson had declared

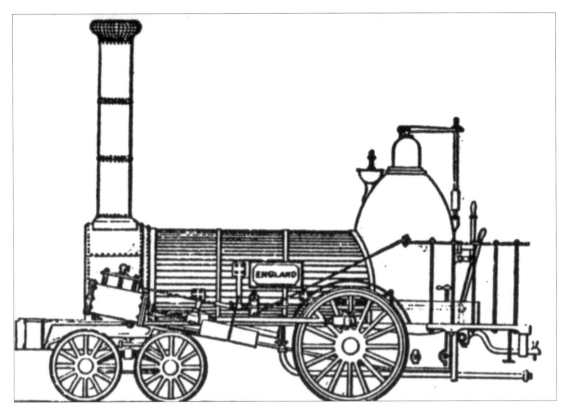

4-2-0 *England* built by William Norris, Philadelphia, in 1839 for the BGR. (*Author's collection*)

Norris A Extra class 4-2-0 *Philadelphia* climbing the Lickey Incline, c. 1841. (*From a painting by F. J. Dolby*)

Gradient post at the foot of the Lickey Incline, 16 April 1953. (*Dr A. J. G. Dickens*)

locomotives impracticable on this steep section, but Moorsom had seen engines in the USA tackling such gradients and placed an order with Norris, locomotive builders of Philadelphia.

On 17 April 1839, a bill was presented to Parliament seeking powers to borrow cash against the security of the works completed to date. Worcester, outraged at being left off the line, sent John Hill, its town clerk, to oppose the bill, attempting to use this as a lever until the railway company agreed to complete the Worcester branch before the main line. In view of Hill's demands, the BGR withdrew its bill, Worcester having to be content with a horse bus service from the BGR station at Spetchley until Midland Railway trains were able to reach it over Oxford, Worcester & Wolverhampton metals on 5 October 1850.

By June 1839, the line was 'in a great state of forwardness', while at Gloucester, tenders were invited for 'building an Engine House and Workshops and also for building Offices and other Erections for the Railway Station at Rigby, in the parish of Stoke Prior, near Bromsgrove'. Tenders were sought for 'Ballasting, also Fitting and Laying of the Permanent Way' between Tibberton (near Worcester) and Ashchurch (near Tewkesbury), amounting to about 14 miles in length of double way. Good progress was being made with the Tewkesbury branch and it was said that station reflected great credit on the contractor F. P. Holder.

Little is recorded about construction workers. Boys were employed to drive the horse-drawn trams to carry spoil from excavations to form embankments. When full, a horse got up speed, was detached and the tram rolled to the end of the embankment where it was tipped. The ground could become very slippery with wet clay, and it was all too easy to fall down. William Clifford, aged thirteen, and Frederick Edwin and Augustus Holland, both fourteen, were killed when run over by trams. The death of

Holland was particularly sad, as his parents lost not only a son, but their chief means of living, when they no longer received his 14s a week in wages.

On 13 July 1839, the Cheltenham paper, *The Looker On*, reported,

UNFASHIONABLE ARRIVAL! On Tuesday last. [9 July] at noon, the first Locomotive Railway Engine ever seen in Cheltenham, made its appearance in the High Street, exciting considerable attention as it passed along, drawn by twelve horses, on a carriage apparently prepared for that especial purpose. The lustrous stranger was conveyed along the Promenade and through the new opening near the Queen's Hotel, into the Old Well Lane and thence to the railway of the Cheltenham and Great Western Union, at the end of Lansdown Place. This engine has been provided by the contractor, Mr Oldham, for the purpose of more rapidly and effectually proceeding with the works along the line, upon which it is expected to be in full operation on Monday, commencing its leviathan labours about two miles from the proposed depot. We observed it was very appropriately named *The Excavator* and we have been informed its weight is between eleven and twelve tons.

In August 1839 four locomotives had been delivered, thirty-five wagons were in the depot at Bromsgrove (BGR stations were called 'depots'), Tewkesbury depot was ready and that at Cheltenham almost complete. By the end of November, works in the neighbourhood of Cheltenham were progressing satisfactorily, the station was in a forward state, and *The Excavator* at work ballasting between the town and Ashchurch. The directors were expecting to make a trial run over the line in early December, but the incessant rain at the end of the year and the beginning of 1840 delayed the anticipated opening of the BGR as the wetness made it necessary to halt construction on two to four days every week in order not to cause injury to the earthworks, which generally remained firm despite the conditions, only two slips occurring in cuttings and one on an embankment. Apart from some delay through the tardiness of the kyanising contractor (kyanising was a wood preserving process), Samuel Bowly, who was also the deputy chairman of the BGR, the supply of permanent way materials was in advance of the building contractor's demands and 19 miles had been laid. Ten locomotives had been delivered, three of which were employed in forming the embankment in the Rea Valley near Birmingham and the remainder used as required in conveying materials, chiefly between Bredon, Tewkesbury and Cheltenham.

On 11 March 1840, Mary Irons, aged sixty-nine, was returning across the line at Churchdown with a pail of water. She was gazing at an engine drawing twenty-three contractors' wagons, and failed to see that seven had been uncoupled and were approaching on the rail on which she stood. Her deafness prevented her from hearing them and they struck her down. She was placed on a door and taken to Cheltenham, but died on the way.

On 16 March 1840, the directors inspected Cheltenham station and proceeded by rail to Ashchurch. Trial runs were made between Cheltenham and Eckington in May and June 1840. Herbert Spencer records an incident with the Norris engines: 'In the afternoon we happened to have two engines going the same way on the two lines of rails and a race was the consequence; we went side by side at between 30–40 mph for a mile or so and shook hands from one train to another.'

On 1 May 1840, the engine *Worcester* left Tewkesbury with a train of ballast wagons loaded with rails, and after dropping them at Bredon, returned to reload. When within a third of a mile of Tewkesbury, driver Joseph Howden, knowing that the impetus would carry the train to the station, let off steam and filled the boiler with water. Unfortunately, a wagon blocked the line. In order to halt the engine was reversed, but having no steam, could not stop. Two men in a wagon being propelled by the engine were killed. The driver was found to be drunk and charged with manslaughter.

When Captain Melluish inspected the BGR on behalf of the Board of Trade, he discovered that Down trains used Birmingham clock times and Up trains used Cheltenham time, one being ten minutes and the other fifteen minutes later than London time. He recommended that all railways should adopt London time, under the apellation of 'railway time'.

On 1 June 1840, a party of directors travelling in two coaches and four wagons inspected the line. They left Cheltenham at 9.00 a.m. and after stopping at Eckington, reached Spetchley at 10.00 a.m. Resuming their journey fifteen minutes later, they arrived Bromsgrove at 10.41 a.m. and were met by

> an excellent band provided by Mr Baylis, one of the subcontractors [actually the Resident engineer], who also furnished a number of flags, and as the party took the musicians, banners etc. with them on their return, the train assumed a very gay appearance, and led to the supposition that it was a public opening of the line, which opinion was further strengthened by the fact that five carriages, also accompanied with music and banners, containing shareholders and other parties interested in the great undertaking residing in Tewkesbury, joined the train at Ashchurch. After a brief stay at Bromsgrove the train returned to Cheltenham, and then again performed the journey to and fro. (*Gloucester Journal*)

On 15 June 1840, an auction held at Stoke Prior sold surplus material such as tools, barrows and timber left over from construction.

The 31 miles of line from Bromsgrove to Cheltenham were opened for passenger traffic on 24 June 1840, some two weeks earlier than expected – an unusual occurrence, as many railways tended to open late due to 'unforeseen difficulties'. The first train consisted of two first- and two second-class coaches drawn by Norris 4-2-0 No. 11 *W. S. Moorsom*, leaving ten minutes late at 9.10 a.m., 'quickly receding from the astonished gaze of the persons assembled'. It arrived at Ashchurch at 9.26 a.m. and left 3½ minutes later. After accelerating from Bredon, 'an excellent pace was maintained – at least 30 mph'. Eckington, 12 miles from Cheltenham, was reached at 9.45 a.m., having averaged 24 mph including stops. At the station, 'passengers flocking to ride upon a train for the very first time in their lives, crammed the carriages to capacity. When the train reached Spetchley, road coaches were waiting to take up passengers for Worcester, this stop also being used to enable the engine to take on water' (*Cheltenham Chronicle*). At

Birmingham and Gloucester Railway.

NOTICE IS HEREBY GIVEN, that on and after WEDNESDAY NEXT, the 24th of June, the portion of this RAILWAY between Cheltenham and the Station near Bromsgrove, will be OPEN for the conveyance of Passengers, Parcels, Carriages, and Horses.

Until further notice there will be only two Trains each way per day, viz. :—

From Bromsgrove Station.............. 10½ A.M. and 7 P.M.
From Cheltenham .... 9 A.M. ... 6 P.M.
No trains will run on Sundays at present.

Arrangements have been made to work Road Coaches between the Station near Bromsgrove and Birmingham, by which a limited number of Passengers can be booked through from Cheltenham to Birmingham; and also, by application at the Swan, Hen and Chickens, Nelson, and Castle Hotel Coach Offices, from Birmingham to Cheltenham. The Coaches for the above Trains will leave Birmingham at 8½ A.M. and 5 P.M. The Fares between Birmingham and Cheltenham are—First Class, 11s. 6d.; Second, 8s.

It is expected that the Line will be further opened to within eleven miles of Birmingham early in July, when additional Trains will be put on and arrangements made to convey Passengers, &c., between Birmingham and Exeter, and all intermediate places, in one day.

Gentlemen's Carriages and Horses must be at the Stations at least a quarter of an hour before the time of departure of the Trains.   By order.
                                        WILLIAM BURGESS,
Dated June 17th, 1840.   Superintendent and Secretary.

Notice in the *Gloucester Journal* advertising the opening of the BGR between Cheltenham and Bromsgrove, 24 June 1840.

BIRMINGHAM & GLOUCESTER RAILWAY.

Fast Day and Night Coaches
FROM THE
LION HOTEL COACH OFFICE, BATH,
TO

BIRMINGHAM .... Daily at 12 o'Clock
☞ Arriving at 9 o'Clock in the Evening.
BIRMINGHAM .... Evenings at 6 o'Clock
MANCHESTER }
        AND   } .... Evenings at 6 o'Clock
LIVERPOOL..
CHELTENHAM } .... Daily at 12 o'Clock
        AND   }   and
WORCESTER } .... Evenings at 6.
-LONDON COACHES SIX TIMES A-DAY,
                    WM. LANE, *Proprietor.*

Notice in the *Bath & Cheltenham Gazette,* 14 July 1840, advertising a journey from Bath to Birmingham utilising the newly-opened BGR.

10.50 a.m., the train arrived at Bromsgrove, passengers for Birmingham continuing by road. Coach travel was included in the rail fare, but two guards were sacked for telling passengers that they needed to pay for the coach. At 10.55 a.m., the train left Bromsgrove for its return run and reached Cheltenham at 12.27 p.m. The *Cheltenham Chronicle* reporter noted that 'Bridges which cross the line are very neat, being open woodwork, in imitation of the heavier iron bridges'.

Receipts on the first day were £91 2s 9d and each successive day showed increasing amounts; on 14 July, takings were £170 15s 9d, or upwards of £1,000 per week since the train service was inaugurated. Passenger traffic was nearly double the estimated figure. Up to 30 June, an average of 4,092 passengers were carried weekly.

In 1838, twenty-two road coaches had carried 2,122 passengers weekly from Cheltenham to Bromsgrove, whereas in July 1840 the number of passengers carried by rail each week was 4,092. Of the twenty-two coaches, eleven were still on the road in August 1840, carrying a fair number of passengers.

Passengers were banned from smoking on railway property; the staff was expected to be polite and helpful and not expect tips for services rendered. In the event of a train being full, long-distance passengers were to be given priority. Staff for the locomotive department were recruited for their technical skill, but all other staff were recruited as Special Constables and initially responsible to civil magistrates. After the line had opened and its by-laws had been approved by the Board of Trade, they were then responsible to the company.

On joining, each man was required to repeat and sign: 'I - - - being this day engaged as - - - in the service of the Birmingham and Gloucester Railway do hereby bind myself to observe and obey the foregoing regulations.' Pay was attractive – 18s weekly compared to the 10–15s earned by a farm worker. In due course, the constables specialised and became brakesmen, clerks, guards, inspectors, shunters, switchmen and so on, in addition to those bobbies who patrolled the line and regulated traffic. A policeman's uniform cost £6 8s 3d in 1839 – in other words, about a month and a half's pay.

At the principal stations, at least one man was to be on duty to 'prevent every species of disorder, direct the passengers, and to see that no loose characters idle and lounge about'. In October 1840, all employees were informed that the company would enforce the Railways Act of 1840 regarding safety, and that the slightest infringement of railway rules would render the offender liable to dismissal and prosecution. This strict order probably accounts for the fact that the BGR had an excellent safety record compared with its contemporaries.

Each train had three members of staff: two guards and a travelling porter. The first guard was in overall charge and was required to check the brakes, lamps and cleanliness of the train before it left the originating station. He was responsible for seeing that passengers were in their proper seats,were not smoking and were behaving in a seemly fashion. He was to apply brakes on hearing the brake whistle. The second guard was to assist him in all these duties, while the porter provided more brake power when required and assisted station porters in helping passengers in and out of the coaches. In the interests of economy, the luxury of three men to a train did not last long.

BGR fares were among the highest in the country. One gentleman took his family from Spetchley to Birmingham (27 miles) at a cost of £4 9s 0d and then travelled onwards to Leamington, another 27 miles, for only £2 12s 6d. Convicts were carried, six or more in a horse box, at third-class fares.

Captain Moorsom founded a benevolent fund, workmen paying a small subscription and being able to claim sickness benefit and medical fees. Fines collected from the company's servants were also paid into this fund, it benefitting to the sum of £8 6s 2d for misdemeanours perpetrated in the last half of 1841.

Although employees were dismissed, they were sometimes reinstated. For example, Thomas Enoch was given the sack for alleged rudeness to a passenger. He then appeared at Spetchley, employed as assistant station clerk with pay of 25s a week; when the stationmaster left, he was given the vacant position.

If an honest passenger lost a ticket he was treated the same as a fraudulant one – a fine of £2 and payment of the full Birmingham to Gloucester fare of 7s 6d. A writer to *Herapath's Railway Journal* in 1843 observed that passengers seemed to sit anywhere and no one checked whether they had the correct class of ticket, only when they were arriving at the two termini.

Trains were regulated by policemen displaying flags by day and lamps at night. White indicated Clear; green warned Caution while red meant Stop. Red would be displayed for five minutes after the passing of a train; then white would be shown, but after ten minutes the line was assumed to be clear. By 1843, disc signals had been introduced. When the GWR opened between Gloucester and Cheltenham, a serious problem arose at Tramway Junction east of Gloucester station. To a GWR driver, a red disc meant go, while to a BGR driver it meant Stop. To avoid this problem, in 1846 Stevens & Son supplied some of their patent semaphore signals. Nineteen were purchased for £383 and used between Gloucester and Birmingham.

Drivers communicated with guards via the whistle: a short blast alerted the guard; three short blasts ordered application of the brakes; while a long blast indicated release them.

In October 1840, it was announced that the BGR anticipated opening to Gloucester early in November as the works on the unopened section were 'in great forwardness' and would be completed before the end of the month. Improvements were being carried out to Lansdown station in order to cope with the extension. The line was opened on 4 November 1840, and despite a 'pitiless storm' 1,500 people were present at 7.30 a.m. when the first train left. One train in the afternoon carried 100 passengers. By December, approximately 2,000 passengers travelled between Cheltenham and Gloucester each week.

The *Gloucester Chronicle* reported that, 'The station, a large wooden structure with a great extent of roofing, has been erected with extraordinary rapidity. At the starting of the twelve o'clock train, the fields, the road, every nook and corner, in short anywhere contiguous to the line and favourable for catching a sight of the huge carriages as they whizzed along, were covered with spectators, of all ages and classes. The passengers very generally have borne testimony to the comfort of the carriages and the peculiarly easy motion of the line'. The train used by the reporter travelled to Cheltenham at an average speed of approximately 31 mph while the return was at 26 mph. Apart from mail trains required by the GPO, no trains were run on Sundays. The line between Bromsgrove and Cofton Farm was opened on 17 September 1840, a temporary station being built near the south end of the tunnel.

Today it is difficult to realise what a great event a train journey was for the early Victorians. Rachel Whinyates, in October 1840, wrote in her diary regarding a departure from Cheltenham, 'Got up early to see Laetitia off. We went to the train station at a little after 7 o'clock and at 8 the strange and wonderful steam conveyance set off, moving slowly at first. The carriages are very comfortable like armchairs, for six persons each. At Birmingham (50 miles in 3 hours) they enter a fresh train for Liverpool. One cannot but feel nervous. God grant a safe arrival.'

Unfortunately, a fatal accident befell a passenger travelling on a coach linking Cofton Farm with the centre of Birmingham. Horses were changed at *The Bell*, Northfield, passengers taking the opportunity to stretch their legs. A lady was just about to enter the coach when a noise startled the horses, causing them to bolt. She was run over by the wheels and died two days later.

A groom assisted loading two animals into a horse box standing in a siding at Bromsgrove station. When the Down train arrived, it was being manhandled to the main line when it was struck by a light engine causing it to go in the reverse direction. The groom fell under the horse box and died of his injuries three days later.

On behalf of the Board of Trade, Sir Frederick Smith inspected the line from Cofton Farm to Camp Hill and was not impressed. Cuttings at Longbridge and Groveley were unfinished and the slopes each side, especially at Groveley were 'rugged and precipitous'. Some of the lofty embankments did not appear to be safely consolidated. The Camp Hill terminus was unfinished lacking some rails and all the signals. He recommended that the opening be postponed, but if not, a 10 mph speed limit be imposed.

The directors, knowing they were not legally bound to adhere to the inspector's report, informed the Board of Trade that they were unable to defer the opening. Cuttings were tidied, a policeman stationed at Groveley to warn of any slips and with no celebrations the line opened to the public on 17 December 1840. The secretary, William Burgess, made an inspection with the resident engineer, F. H. P. Wetherall, and said that Groveley cutting appeared unsafe and might slip at any moment. He suggested that land on each side be purchased to widen cutting and decrease the slope. His suggestion was adopted. When the line opened throughout on 17 December 1840 the rails were covered with a heavy fall of snow, but trains were only a few minutes late.

The railway enabled a forger to be apprehended. On 29 April 1841, George Comley, his wife and six children caught the 11.00 a.m. train from Gloucester to Birmingham as they were emigrating from North Nibley, near Dursley, to the USA via Liverpool. Soon after their train left, W. Gillman of North Nibley arrived in the hope of intercepting Comley, who had executed a forgery on him to the extent of £40 in addition to other frauds.

After consulting with police Superintendent Walker, on payment of £10 an engine was prepared which, with Gillman and Superintendent Walker on the footplate, sped after the train which had a twenty minute start. They caught sight of the train at Ashchurch and followed close in its wake – no divisions into sections then – and at Spetchley, much to the surprise and consternation of Comley, he was caught by his pursuers. On arrival at Birmingham, Gillman gave him into police custody. On Superintendent Walker's return to Gloucester, he found Comleys's landlord, who had too late tried to embargo his luggage. Comley had been carrying out a clothier business at North Nibley until he suddenly decamped. He was returned to Gloucester for trial; his wife returned to North Nibley while his children were left in Birmingham. He was sentenced to Gloucester prison for debt.

In July 1841, it was reported that traffic on the Gloucester to Cheltenham turnpike road had so decreased following the opening of the railway that tolls were insufficient to maintain the road in good repair.

The exterior of Curzon Street station, Birmingham, *c.* 1839. (*J. C. Bourne*)

Curzon Street station. (*Author's collection*)

The interior of the former Grand Junction Railway passenger station at Curzon Street in use as a goods depot, 14 May 1939. Coaches from the London & Birmingham Railway were transferred through the opening, right. (*B. Brierley*)

On 14 August 1841, Sir Frederick Smith inspected the extension from Camp Hill to the London & Birmingham's new Curzon Street station. He was concerned about safety at the junction of two main lines and recommended that trains stop before proceeding over the junction. The line opened to the public on 17 August 1841.

The six months' rent payable for the use of the London & Birmingham's Curzon Street station amounted to £500, the original Camp Hill station being relegated to goods use from this date. The opening to Curzon Street, which had a station hotel and a smaller echo of the Doric arch at Euston at the other end of the London & Birmingham's line, meant that there was now a continuous line of railway between York, Hull, Leeds, Sheffield, Derby, Nottingham, Leicester, London, Liverpool, Manchester and Gloucester. It was the fact that it enjoyed easy access from all parts of the country that helped Cheltenham develop as an important educational centre. On 15 November that year, Camp Hill was partly reopened to passengers as the 3.30 p.m. departure and the 1.40 p.m. and 7.10 p.m. arrivals were goods trains that also carried passengers. The *Bristol Standard* criticised a very sharp curve near the junction with the London & Birmingham, and said that everything depended on the brakes and carefulness of the drivers and guards. Two wagons of coke 'flew over the embankment'.

To enable through trains from Derby and Bristol to avoid a reversal at Birmingham, a direct link was made in 1864 between the former Birmingham & Derby Junction line at Landon Street Junction to the former Birmingham & Gloucester at St Andrew's Junction. Portions of trains running to or from Birmingham were marshalled at Camp Hill or Saltley, running to New Street, the new central station opened by the London & North Western Railway on 1 June 1854.

BIRMINGHAM AND GLOUCESTER RAILWAY.

ALTERATION OF TRAINS.

ON and AFTER MONDAY, the 2nd of MAY, this Company's TRAINS will RUN as follows, until further notice :—

FROM BIRMINGHAM.	FROM GLOUCESTER.
H. M.	H. M.
12 44 a.m. (Mail)	† †
3 10 a.m. (Mail)	8 15 a.m.
* *	11 15 a.m.
* 8 45 a.m.	2 0 p.m.
12 15 p.m.	4 30 p.m.
2 45 p.m.	7 15 p.m. (Mail)
6 15 p.m.	9 0 p.m. (Mail)

☞ * Goods Train, carrying 1st, 2nd, and 3rd Class Passengers, from Camp Hill, Birmingham, to Gloucester, 5 30 a.m.
† † Goods Train, carrying 1st, 2nd, and 3rd Class Passengers, from Gloucester to Camp Hill, Birmingham, 5 30 a.m.
Passengers may be booked in London, for Worcester, Cheltenham, and Gloucester, by Trains leaving the London Station of the London and Birmingham Railway, at 6 and 9¼ a.m.; and from those places, for London, by the Trains leaving Gloucester at 8¼ a.m., and 2 and 9 p.m.

By order,   GEORGE KING, Secretary.
12, Waterloo-street, Birmingham, April 19, 1842.   (4351)

Timetable amendment dated 19 April 1842.

MR trains ran to this station from 1 July when Curzon Street closed to regular passenger traffic, the 1836 BGR Act stipulating regarding the London & Birmingham Railway that the BGR should have entry to 'any future terminus of that company in or near Birmingham'.

On 3 April 1876, the MR opened a new line, the West Suburban Railway, from New Street Junction to King's Norton via Selly Oak. The need for engines to run round at New Street was obviated from 1 October 1885 when MR expresses travelled via the West Suburban Railway, thus enabling them to use New Street without need for a reversal.

Because of the lack of sidings on the BGR, freight was conveyed to only a limited extent at first, though the principal carriers (firms that arranged for goods to be carried) were prepared to commence using the BGR as soon as it could accommodate them. Goods traffic began in October 1841, an experimental load of coal being sent to Cheltenham, but it was believed that unless return traffic could be obtained, it would not prove remunerative. The trial was a success, and in July 1842 Mr Williams rented the wharf at Alstone Lane, Cheltenham, soon expanding by opening wharves at Spetchley, Eckington, Bredon and Ashchurch and purchasing a fleet of wagons for his own use. A smart move was that his empty coal wagons returned north with general goods at a discounted rate.

The BGR did not go all out to seek freight traffic, but passively waited for it to come. An estimate of the Severn trade between Gloucester and Worcester was 585,000 tons annually, yet in 1842 the BGR carried only 29,000 tons. It was acknowledged that until the Bristol & Gloucester Railway was opened, much of the traffic would remain waterborne.

In February 1844, the directors adopted the system of becoming their own carriers. This proved beneficial as an increase in goods traffic could not have occurred while the carriers were more interested in water than rail conveyance and had the power of turning traffic from one to the other as best suited their purpose. For example, in April 1842, Messrs Crowley & Co. sent a consignment of casks of porter from Bristol to Dudley. They specified that rail transport be used between Gloucester and Birmingham, yet it travelled by water. The carrier claimed he had made a 'mistake'. When the customer found that his goods took just as long by 'rail' as by water, he reverted to water. The low depth of the Severn during the summer of 1844 made water transport difficult, and facilitated the efforts of the BGR in obtaining goods traffic.

Goods trains were restricted to sixteen loaded wagons and accommodation for third-class passengers, while a first- and second-class composite catered for the others. These trains were supplemented by an extra goods-only train if required for coal, empty wagons and company stores. A guard had a travelling porter to assist him in braking, shunting and loading and fire-watching. The latter was important, as in October 1841 a cinder ignited a tarpaulin and a load of lace and cloth was damaged, requiring compensation of £120 which had to be paid from the six months' takings of £590.

Captain Constantine Richard Moorsom RN (not to be confused with his Army namesake, the engineer) was elected to the board of directors in January 1841 and, before accepting, expressed his views on the desirability of further reducing the number of directors to three or five, from the twelve to which it had been cut in 1837. Moorsom believed that, with his overall assistance, each director should be held directly responsible for a particular department. This modification in executive structure was essential as the slump of 1841/42 had caused receipts to fall and operating expenses to soar to 62 per cent of gross revenue; additionally, liabilities of £172,000 had been discovered, requiring the raising of £175,000.

During the first six months of 1842, fewer passengers travelled than during the same period the previous year. On the brighter side, goods traffic was increasing, but rail, as opposed to horse tramway, communication was required to Gloucester docks and an irregularity was experienced in the transport of goods onwards to Bristol. Level crossing gatekeepers, hitherto a source of expenditure, brought in revenue when most of the crossings were turned into stations.

In the first half of 1843, the number of passengers carried fell by 6¼ per cent due to increased fares charged for first- and second-class passengers. A special meeting of the proprietors was held on 13 January 1843 in compliance with a requisition to the directors signed by nearly a thousand shareholders, for the purpose of 'considering and determining as to the appointment of a committee of shareholders, *not being* directors, of the said Company,' who should ascertain the state of the BGR financially, materially and otherwise. In the course of discussion it was declared that the estimated cost of the line had been largely exceeded and that there had been many mistakes in its administration. One critic said that at High Orchard, Gloucester, was a wet basin

> so ingeniously constructed as to be fed by a stream of water which is fast filling it up with mud, and so admirably situated as to be inaccessible. The presumption would be that this is a receptacle intended for traffic, and that it will be surrounded by sheds and warehouses for the reception of goods, but the only buildings contiguous are six large coke ovens, which are not at work because the coke could be contracted for elsewhere on better terms. The wet basin is a melancholy spectacle; especially when it is considered that at the bottom of its foul waters lie something like £14,000 of our money.

The result of this discussion was the formation of a Committee of Enquiry to consist of four proprietors and three directors. This was seen as a victory for both sides, but two of the proprietors later became directors. Matters improved, and example being locomotive expenses of 2s 10d a mile in 1840 had fallen to 1s a mile in 1841, so a dividend of 1¼ per cent was declared.

The Committee of Enquiry made economies and early in 1843 eleven switchmen were discharged and their duties replaced by locomotive firemen. Those who were retained were 'screwed down to the starving point of 11s to 16s per week' – *Railway Times & Record*. A staff of 719 in August 1841 was reduced to 271 by March 1843, saving some £4,000 per annum. Passenger traffic was only two-thirds of that expected when the Act was sought, but the committee believed it would rise dramatically when the Cheltenham & Great Western Union Railway and the Bristol & Gloucester Railway were open. Freight too would improve.

Captain Moorsom resigned chairmanship in December 1843 and his deputy, Samuel Bowly, took over. Bowly was also chairman of the Anti-Dry Rot Company which kyanised timber. Humphrey Brown was appointed traffic manager and said he would work without salary until his plans gave the proprietors a dividend of 3 per cent. Matters improved in the second half of 1843, a profit of almost £14,000 being made, a dividend of 1½ per cent declared and working expenses reduced from 90 per cent of revenue to 75 per cent. Locomotive expenses had fallen to 10½d a mile and claimed only 10 per cent of the working expenses instead of the 30–40 per cent previously. Weekly receipts from goods traffic improved from £246 in June 1843 to £1,056 in June 1844.

Coal was sent in both directions on the BGR: from the Forest of Dean and South Wales to the Birmingham gasworks, and from Birmingham to Cheltenham (up to 100 tons daily). In 1844, arrangements were made with the Grand Junction, Birmingham & Derby and Manchester & Birmingham railways for the reciprocal interchange of goods traffic without the delay and expense of shifting by hand.

The opening of the Bristol & Gloucester Railway on 8 July 1844 brought extra traffic to the line, though introduced a break of gauge, as the Bristol line was broad gauge. Bowly said, 'The best understanding has existed between the Directors of this company and those of the Bristol & Gloucester Company and they are cordially acting together for their mutual interests and the convenience of the public.' The Birmingham & Gloucester station was alongside, but just south of the Bristol & Gloucester station, the two gauges crossing on the level about a quarter of a mile from the termini.

It was reported that the number of passengers travelling on the BGR had been reduced by the number of road coaches put on between Worcester and Oxford following the opening of the GWR to Oxford on 12 June 1844, but it was hoped that the anticipated reduction of fares on the London & Birmingham line would speedily restore traffic to its former level.

Toward the end of 1844, an important event occurred. Terms for the union of the Bristol and Birmingham companies were reached, it making much sense to have one company working throughout. On 7 January 1845 the Birmingham & Gloucester prepared a draft resolution for immediate amalgamation on the terms, 'All assets, liabilities and engagements of the two companies to be taken by the united companies.'

This was followed by a Heads of Agreement made on 14 January 1845 between the respective chairmen, the principal points including:

1)   The two companies to be united under the title Bristol & Birmingham Railway and an Act of Parliament to be applied for to ratify this.

2)   Until the Act is obtained, the affairs of the two companies to be administered by a board of management with fourteen members – seven from each board. The chairman to be chosen by the Birmingham & Gloucester board.

3)   After the passing of the Act, the board to be elected by the proprietors of the united companies.

4)   The stock of the united company to be £1,800,000: £1,142,125 belonging to the shareholders of the Birmingham & Gloucester and £657,875 to the Bristol & Gloucester.

MIDLAND RAILWAY.—Notice is hereby Given, that a Special General Meeting of the Proprietors of the Midland Railway Company will be held at the Railway Station at Derby, on Saturday, the 12th day of April next, at Two o'clock in the Afternoon, for the purpose of confirming or otherwise a certain agreement entered into between the Birmingham and Gloucester Railway Company and the Bristol and Gloucester Railway Company of the one part, and the Midland Railway Company of the other part, for the granting of a lease in perpetuity to the Midland Railway Company of the Birmingham and Gloucester and Bristol and Gloucester Railways, at an annual rent equivalent to 6 per cent. on the united share capital of those railways, with such provisions for the working of these railways and such other provisions as are contained in the said agreement, or as may be deemed expedient and for other special purposes.—Dated this 26th day of March, 1845.

GEORGE HUDSON, Chairman } Of the Board
JOHN ELLIS, Deputy Chairman } of Directors.
By Order,
J. F. BELL, Secretary.

A bill to constitute the Bristol & Birmingham Railway Company was made, but withdrawn after the second reading through failure to comply with Standing Orders, though in lieu of amalgamation the lines were worked as one until the Midland took over on 7 May 1845.

Immediately after the agreement had been signed, the GWR invited the company to negotiate on extending the broad gauge to Birmingham, as it believed that there was an absolute necessity for a uniform gauge from the Midlands to Bristol. These meetings resulted in a proposal to amalgamate with the GWR. On 24 January 1845 the Great Western offered Birmingham & Gloucester shareholders £60 of GWR capital, then worth £123, for each £100 of Birmingham & Gloucester worth £109. The Bristol and Birmingham companies held out for £65 and the meeting was deferred until 27 January.

On 26 January, by pure chance, John Ellis, deputy chairman of the Midland Railway, travelled to London in the same compartment as Edward Sturge and Joseph Gibbons, the Birmingham directors going to the meeting. They promised him that if they did not find satisfaction with the GWR, they would bargain with him and on his own responsibility pledged his company to take perpetual lease of the Bristol & Birmingham at an annual rent of 6 per cent and undertake all outstanding liabilities. On 27 January, Charles Saunders, secretary of the GWR, said that his company could not increase its offer, so the Bristol & Birmingham turned to Ellis.

On 30 January 1845, an agreement was officially made between Samuel Bowly, Edward Sturge and John Ellis to lease the Bristol & Birmingham. Whateley, the Birmingham & Gloucester's solicitor, sent the following letter to Osborne, his Bristol counterpart:

Carlton Club, 30th January 1845.

My Dear Osborne,

The Midland Company have agreed through Mr Ellis the Deputy Chairman to take all our liabilities and to take a lease of our line from Birmingham to Bristol at 6 per cent on £1,800,000 for 14 years at least.

On Monday the agreement is to be settled, but these terms are finally agreed upon. The Great Western were previously seen by Bowly, and unhesitatingly refused to give the £65.

Yours very sincerely,

George Whateley.

A further Heads of Agreement was made. Under the conviction of the absolute necessity for a single gauge between the Midlands and Bristol,

it is now agreed that a lease in perpetuity of the Birmingham & Gloucester and Bristol & Gloucester shall be forthwith granted to the Midland Railway Company on the following terms:

It is understood that the amalgamation of the two first mentioned companies agreed to on the 14 January is to be considered and carried into effect.

The Midland Railway to pay to the united Birmingham and Bristol Companies an annual rent equivalent to six per cent on their united share capital of £1,800,000.

The Midland Railway Company to undertake all liabilities and engagements of the two other companies which liabilities up to the present time are estimated to amount to about £457,000.

The Stock of Engines, Carriages and all other property and effects of the Birmingham and Bristol companies to become the property of the Midland Company.

The Midland's perpetual lease of the Bristol & Birmingham Railway (BBR) was to commence on 1 July 1845. The MR had powers to purchase the two railways on payment of £150 for £100 stock at any time after the expiration of three years following the commencement of the lease. George Hudson, the Midland's chairman, speaking at Derby on 12 August 1845 said, 'I can take no credit myself, gentlemen, for having originated this arrangement. My friend, Mr Ellis, to whom I wish to give all the credit, which is so justly his due, suggested to the Board this bold course.'

The second amalgamation scheme rendered the first unnecessary, but it was decided to let both go before Parliament so that if one case failed, they could fall back on the other. Thus in 1846 there were two bills before the House relating to the BBR. The first was to consolidate the two companies, this bill being read the first time on 17 March 1846 while two days later, a bill vesting the Bristol & Gloucester in the MR was also read for this first time. On 27 March both bills were read a second time and the former bill was dropped. The Midland Amalgamation Act, 9–10 Victoria cap 326, received royal assent on 3 August 1846.

It stated that the share capital of the Birmingham & Gloucester Railway consisted of 9,374 shares of £100 and 8,189 of £25; while the share capital of the Bristol & Gloucester was 7,539 shares of £50. The MR was authorised to create 9,374 new shares of £100 each, 7,539 of £50, 7,539 of £37 5s 0d and 8,189 of £25. Birmingham & Gloucester shareholders were to receive the same number of MR shares, Bristol & Gloucester £50 shareholders receiving the same number of MR £50 6 per cent shares, and were additionally entitled to a like number of MR 6 per cent £37 5s 0d shares, subject to payment of that amount and 4½ per cent interest from 1 July 1845.

The first meeting of the BBR had been held on 14 February 1845 when Samuel Bowly was elected chairman. Burgess and Harding were joint superintendents, coming respectively from the Birmingham and Bristol lines, and were directed to take immediate measures for working the whole line from Bristol to Birmingham as an entity and to develop its resources. Revenue from the Bristol to Gloucester section (Gloucester itself being excluded) was to be paid to the Bristol bankers and the rest to those at Birmingham.

On 6 May 1845, two Bristol directors and two Birmingham directors retired in order that four Midland directors could be appointed, these four taking over the entire management of the Bristol & Gloucester and Birmingham & Gloucester from 7 May 1845. Wyndham Harding, the Bristol superintendent who had done so well for his company, left the same day to take up a post on the London & Birmingham Railway.

On 7 May 1845, the Board of Trade issued a statement regarding the amalgamation saying, 'We are not prepared to report that we see any sufficient public reasons against allowing the proposed amalgamation of the Birmingham & Gloucester and the Bristol & Gloucester Railway companies, and the lease of the two lines to the Midland Company, in the event of Parliament being of the opinion that the extension of the narrow gauge, rather than of the wide gauge, is to be desired.'

The London & North Western Railway, anxious to keep the Great Western out of the Midlands, undertook to share any loss the Midland made by its purchase of the two companies, this aid being subsequently altered into permission for the MR to use New Street station, Birmingham, for a nominal £100 annually. When the MR took over the Bristol and Birmingham lines, the companies were not earning as much as the Midland was paying for them and in the first eighteen months the BBR showed a deficit of £27,500. After this date the accounts of the two lines were not kept separately, so the profitability or otherwise is not known, but a special examination at the end of 1848 showed that the lines had paid their way and from then on were decidedly profitable.

In June 1845, natural economies of the union caused the secretaryship of Robert Fletcher, (Bristol & Gloucester Railway), to be terminated, Joseph Sanders becoming secretary of the BBR. From 6 September 1846, James Edward McConnell, locomotive superintendent of the Birmingham & Gloucester, was put in charge of all locomotives between Birmingham and Bristol.

Between 13–24 July 1846, Samuel Beale, Peyton and J. H. Sanders inspected the line from Birmingham to Bristol and recommended many staffing economies. The seals of the two companies, being no longer required, were destroyed at the

meeting of the board on 26 October 1846. The last meeting of the Bristol &
Birmingham directors took place at Derby on 12 September 1849.

The Midland Railway did not welcome the break of gauge at Gloucester.
Although Daniel Gooch, Locomotive, Carriage & Wagon Superintendent of the
Great Western, had designed methods for transferring goods including schemes
for wheels sliding on their axles and narrow gauge trucks carried on broad
gauge transporter wagons, he 'never had any faith in any of these plans working
in practice'. Brunel had told the Bristol & Gloucester that broad gauge wagons
would hold twice as much as those of the standard gauge. Consequently that
company only had sixty wagons to transport goods brought by the BGR's 400.
Although Brunel was informed that the transfer shed only held three wagons of
each gauge at a time and that this was quite inadequate, he did nothing to alleviate
the situation.

An 'Old Carrier's Petition to the Directors of the Great Western Railway against
the Break of Gauge', only supposedly written by an old carrier, was merely a
disguised argument against the broad gauge. It reasoned,

> A train would probably consist of thirty-five wagons on the Narrow Gauge line and
> despatch would require four men at least to each wagon to remove articles and one
> clerk to every four wagons to mark off goods; thus altogether the expense would
> be tantamount to 2*s* 6*d* per ton; for to transship one such train with anything like
> despatch, would require one hundred and forty porters and nine clerks. It is found
> at Gloucester that to transship the contents of one wagon full of miscellaneous
> merchandise to another from one gauge to the other, takes about an hour, with all
> the force of porters you can put to work upon it!
>
> In the hurry the bricks are miscounted, the slates chipped at the edges, the cheese
> cracked, the ripe fruit and vegetables crushed and spoiled, the chairs, furniture and
> oil cake, cast iron pots, grates and ovens all more or less broken, the coals turned
> into slack, the salt short of weight, sundry bottles of wine deficient and the fish too
> late for market.

The break of gauge was particularly serious in the case of livestock and it was
claimed that the change from one wagon to another deteriorated the quality of
the meat 'very greatly' and it was found impossible 'to compel animals taken from
one carriage to enter another until an interval of repose in the field or stable has
allayed their tremour and alarm'.

A Royal Commission was appointed to look into the gauge question on
11 July 1845, evidence beginning on 6 August. When the Parliamentary Gauge
Committee visited Gloucester to assess the situation for themselves, J. D. Payne,
goods manager of the Birmingham & Gloucester and later general manager of the
South Staffordshire Railway, craftily arranged for two trains already dealt with
to be unloaded to add to the work and confusion, so that the chaos the break of
gauge caused would be the more impressive.

G. P. Neale wrote in *Railway Reminiscences*, 'When the members came to the
scene, they were appalled by the clamour arising from the well-arranged confusion

of shouting out address of consignments, the chucking of packages across from truck to truck, the enquiries for missing articles, the loading, unloading and reloading, which his clever device had brought into operation.'

The Great Western believed that the Commission should have observed the break of gauge at Bristol, not Gloucester, as it was against the BBR's interest for things to have gone smoothly, but the MR had a good case because extending the narrow gauge to Bristol would certainly have greatly reduced transhipment. In the week ending 25 October 1845, almost 700 tons were transshipped at Gloucester, but only 50 tons at Bristol, with a weekly average of 200–300 tons at Gloucester and 40 tons at Bristol. Another saving would have been in locomotives, for the Midland's standard gauge stock would have sufficed and the number of turntables, engine sheds and goods sheds could have been reduced by half. Despite claims by the 'Old Carrier', the transfer of goods at Gloucester took an average of fifty minutes for a 5 ton wagon and cost a maximum of 3*d* a ton. Nineteen extra porters had to be employed for the transshipment and the BBR estimated that the break of gauge cost the company £2,000 a year. On 14 August 1848 an Act of Parliament, 11 & 12 Victoria cap 131, allowed the MR to build an independent line from Gloucester to Stonehouse and mix the gauge to Bristol, the standard gauge metals being first used on 29 May 1854. The Bristol to Highbridge section of the Bristol & Exeter Railway was converted to mixed gauge on 1 June 1875 and on 28 July 1875 the first standard gauge train ran through from Birmingham to Weston-super-Mare.

Queen Victoria herself experienced the break of gauge when she visited Gloucester on 19 September 1849. Cholera was raging in London and it was thought safer for the Royal Family to travel from Balmoral to Osborne via Gloucester. The floor of the MR station where she arrived was covered with a scarlet cloth, a richer carpet being laid where the royal party crossed the platform. The appearance of the somewhat unsightly columns supporting the roof was enhanced by laurel and flowers. By means of the newly invented electric telegraph, information was received by the thousands waiting at Gloucester that the royal train had passed Cheltenham, the *Gloucester Journal* reporter commenting that, 'The masses began to stir and hum with expectation, till amid the clashing of arms, the crashing of music and the loud cheers of the loyal multitude, the train glided alongside the platform.'

Meanwhile, the GWR had completed the Cheltenham & Great Western Union Railway from Swindon to Gloucester, the line opening on 12 May 1845. The BGR withheld the use of Gloucester station for accommodating Great Western traffic in retaliation for alleged 'spiteful acts'. This dog-in-the-manger attitude was hardly unexpected, as the GWR had prevented the Midland Railway, the new owner of the Birmingham to Bristol line, from laying standard gauge between Gloucester and Standish, while another bone of contention was over a payment and the fact that the GWR had set labourers to work on the BGR between Gloucester and Cheltenham without giving the notice to which they were entitled. Public inconvenience was kept to a minimum by a Heads of Agreement:

9th May – It is agreed that any question of account relative to the works between Gloucester and Cheltenham shall be settled forthwith by Mr Brunel and Mr R. Stephenson, with power to appoint an umpire in case of need.

10th May – The Great Western Company desire to work their traffic into the Gloucester station, uninterruptedly, or to use or build upon the vacant land, for their accommodation. The Bristol and Gloucester and the Birmingham and Gloucester Companies object that such working or use might interfere with certain of their existing rights. With the view to obviating any possible inconvenience to the public, it is agreed that the Great Western Railway Company shall work their traffic into the Gloucester station, and use the vacant land until the question shall be determined by law, and with the distinct understanding that such working and use shall in no way prejudice the existing rights or positions of any of the parties under their respective Acts of Parliament, or otherwise. In case the Great Western Railway Company shall place any buildings on the ground, and it shall afterwards be determined that they have not a right to the land, they shall be at liberty to remove them without making any claim upon the Birmingham and Gloucester Company for their value or cost. The above arrangement is not to extend to such part of the station as is now used by the Birmingham and Gloucester Company.

The GWR worked into a platform added to the north side of the BGR terminus, which had been used by the broad gauge Bristol & Gloucester Railway trains since the previous July.

Receipts from passenger fares grew from £65,730 in 1841 to £139,387 in 1846, while goods receipts over the same period more than tripled from £20,054 to £68,679.

The line was proved a vital artery during both world wars, carrying materials southwards to the coast, and imported supplies northwards. During the night of 29/30 August 1940, a suspected unexploded bomb caused the closure of the line at Churchdown for several hours. In the night of 15/16 October 1940, high explosive bombs damaged LMS stock at High Street goods yard, Cheltenham. On 26 March 1941, four high-explosive bombs were dropped on railway property at Gloucester. Of the five people killed, one was an LMS employee and ten of the seriously injured worked for the LMS. Bombs damaged five coaches in the carriage sidings and the turntable road was put out of action as was the LMS Passenger Station signal box. Windows were broken in the 3.05 p.m. Bristol to Sheffield express standing at the platform. At 1.30 a.m. on 17 June 1941, a high-explosive bomb fell close to the main line near Cheltenham, damaging track and telecommunications. Both lines were blocked until 3.15 a.m. (the line had yet to be quadrupled), and then single line working was introduced over the Down line between Churchdown and Hatherley Junction until normal working was resumed at 9.30 a.m.

On 1 January 1923, the MR became part of the LMS, which in turn became the London Midland Region of BR on Nationalisation in 1948, though until 1950, from a point just north of Selly Oak southwards, the line was part of the Western

Transferring goods from one gauge to the other at Gloucester, 1846. The dog appears unhappy at the inconvenience. (*Courtesy: Illustrated London News*)

Region. On 1 February 1958, the line southwards from the 52½-mile post set between Barnt Green and Blackwell was returned to the Western Region.

The West Midlands Passenger Transport Executive (WMPTE) was formed under an Act of 1968. With privatisation, trains on the route were operated by Virgin CrossCountry from March 1997 while Central Trains provided local services for the WMPTE. Due to arson, the start of electric trains in May 1993 was delayed until 12 July. The 25kV wires ran from New Street to Barnt Green and Redditch. The inner two tracks were electrified south of Longbridge and the outer two to the north. Today, local services are worked by London Midland and express services from Birmingham to Gloucester by CrossCountry, while First Great Western use the southern half of the line when running between Worcester and Gloucester.

A disc signal as used on the BGR. When displayed edge-on to a driver it indicates 'Clear', or 'Stop' when the disc faces him. Notice the policeman – they were originally responsible for signalling – lolling outside his hut.

Permanent Way

The Birmingham & Gloucester Railway used the shallow parallel form of rail with a thick bottom web bevelled off at the sides and weighing 56 lb/yd. They were laid in chairs on longitudinal sleepers of American pine in lengths of up to 60 feet, except on embankments over 15 feet in height where cross sleepers of kyanised beech or larch were used. The sleepers received the preserving treatment by the Anti-Dry Rot Company of Gloucester. Captain Moorsom adopted the plan of setting chairs at 5-foot intervals with intermediate saddles to give vertical, but no lateral support. This plan was not successful as lateral oscillations of locomotives caused bulging of the rail between chairs. An unusual feature was that there were no less than seven different kinds of ballast: burnt clay, burnt marl, gravel, sandstone, rock marl and broken stone of both lias and oolite. The railway company looked after the permanent way while Messrs Berwick & Lamb maintained the embankments. When the MR took over the BGR, track was gradually renewed using cross sleepers.

When the GWR's third rail was laid between Gloucester and Cheltenham, the track was on transverse sleepers and 83 lb/yd rail was used. It was inspected on behalf of the Board of Trade by Captain Simmons on 11 October 1847.

The bridges on the line totalled 163, not counting 126 culverts and were numbered from Gloucester. A peculiar latticework bridge was introduced in which the longitudinal sleepers were supported by transverse joists about 6 feet below the top rail of the framing. These joists were placed about 3 feet from centre to centre and had a bearing on each side of the middle rail or band, which ran from one abutment to the other.

At Ashbury the Tewkesbury to Evesham line crosses the Birmingham to Gloucester line on the level. This view was taken in 1954. (*Dr A. J. G. Dickens*)

Chapter Two

Description of the Line

The Birmingham & Gloucester Railway started from Camp Hill terminal station (42 miles 2 chains from Derby), a line branching off at Camp Hill Junction for Gloucester Junction, this spur forming a link with the London & Birmingham Railway east of Curzon Street. On 17 August 1841, Camp Hill terminus was relegated to the goods department, though for a period, certain night goods trains continued to carry passengers from Camp Hill, which finally closed on 7 February 1966. Camp Hill station on the through line was renamed Camp Hill & Balsall Heath in December 1887, reverting to Camp Hill on 1 April 1904, closing temporarily on 27 July 1941 and permanently on 27 November 1946.

The rising gradient of 1 in 280 continuing through Brighton Road (43 miles 5 chains), steepened to 1 in 108 before Moseley (44 miles 23 chains), renamed King's Heath on 1 November 1867 when a new Moseley station opened (43 miles 43 chains). Moseley Tunnel, 166 yards in length, was immediately south of the new Moseley station. It is believed that Moseley was the first open tunnel constructed for a railway as the local authority had the power to require a portion of the line near the village to be in a tunnel. It was considered to be the least expensive plan to make an open cutting and then put in the tunnel brickwork. This was a series of inverts 15 feet apart, placed below the track, with buttress-rings built on the ends of the inverts. The space between these buttresses was then filled with concave walls. The segments gave the appearance of a caterpillar.

Both King's Heath and Brighton Road stations closed temporarily on 27 January 1941 and permanently on 27 November 1946, though goods traffic at King's Heath continued to be dealt with until May 1966. Brighton Road had no goods facilities.

From King's Heath, the line through Hazelwell (45 miles 6 chains) was level. Hazelwell closed to goods on 1 March 1965, though it lost its passenger traffic on the same date as King's Heath. Lifford (46 miles 3 chains) closed to passengers in November 1844, the second station shut on 28 September 1885 being replaced by a third station, which closed temporarily to passengers on 30 September 1940 and permanently on 27 November 1946, remaining open to goods until 6 July 1964.

One Birmingham New Street stationmaster remarked, 'The joy of the station is that if anything goes wrong, there's always some way to get round it.' This is because being placed on a circle, trains going north or south can leave from

Camp Hill, July 1906. A typical Midland Railway running-in board can be seen on the left. (*Author's collection*)

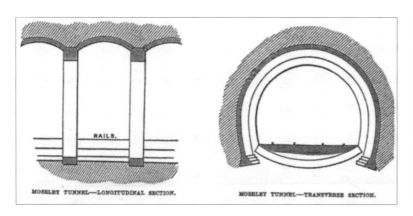
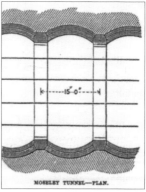

Plan and sections of Moseley Tunnel from *Practical Tunnelling* by F. W. Simms, revised by D. Kinnear Clark, 1877.

Moseley view Down with the tunnel beyond. (*Author's collection*)

Birmingham New Street, *c.* 1905: the LNWR's 1854 station is to the left and the MR's 1885 station on the right. (*Author's collection*)

MR platforms No. 4 and No. 5 at New Street, 1885. The train is for King's Norton via Camp Hill. (*Author's collection*)

Class 2P 4-4-2T No. 2109 built by the MR for the London, Tilbury & Southend section, at New Street, 20 June 1935. (*M. F. Yarwood*)

the opposite direction. Both the MR and LNWR sides of the station were interconnected so that in the event of a blockage on one side of the station, its traffic can be diverted through the other. Until June 1885, all MR expresses between Derby and Bristol avoided New Street by using the Camp Hill line.

When working a Plymouth to Newcastle HST, driver Flower from Bath Road shed, Bristol, at King's Norton found himself wrongly routed via Camp Hill. He stopped, phoned the signalman and was told that there had been a fatality at Selly Oak and this was the reason for the diversion. He restarted the train and rang his guard to inform him of the situation. Guard Gilbert Bailey sounded excited at this news and said he would ring him back. In due course, he told this tale.

On leaving Bristol Parkway, he was going round checking the tickets and was told by an irate lady that her reserved seat was facing the wrong way. Anxious to oblige, guard Bailey offered to move her and her cases to a forward-facing seat, but she was adamant – the seat she was sitting in was hers and there she would remain. As the train was now routed via Camp Hill, it would have to reverse at New Street before proceeding northwards.

On receiving the message from driver Flower, guard Bailey returned to the lady passenger and in a loud voice said that she was quite within her rights and that he'd had a word with the driver and that the driver had agreed to turn the train round. Other passengers murmured that she had been unfair to the guard who had offered her another seat and now had persuaded the poor old driver to turn the train round so that she could face forward!

In April 1876, the Birmingham West Suburban Railway opened from a terminus at Granville Street to Lifford and to this in 1885, the MR laid down double track from New Street to Church Road Junction. To avoid congestion, every effort was made to keep goods traffic out of the station, and in the 1950s, the Midland side only saw four or five goods trains, mainly traffic for Messrs Fry and Cadbury, or, in the season, consignments of fruit from Evesham. Special regulations required that the New Street signal boxes did not accept a freight unless it had a clear road right through the station.

The MR's arrival at New Street required the London & North Western Railway's four-road station to be enlarged. Great Queen Street was taken over and converted to a central carriage drive and beyond this the MR platforms were constructed. Building the line to New Street was difficult and expensive due to having to tunnel below the canal which, to avoid closure during construction of the railway, was carried in temporary wooden troughs. New Street was one of the first centrally-sited stations in the country because, due to the expense of obtaining property, railway stations normally tended to be some distance from a town centre.

Back sidings adjoined the west end of the MR side of New Street. Only a stone's throw from the Birmingham Fish Market, in the 1950s 50–60 tons of fish were unloaded daily, some vans travelling onwards to Gloucester. Although the fish traffic was good for railway finance, it was unpleasant for the noses of passengers waiting on nearby platforms. Theatrical traffic was also handled at Back Sidings.

During an air raid in the Second World War, one fireman shovelled an incendiary bomb off the footplate and then, in the tunnel outside the station,

Rebuilding New Street station, 14 August 1966. (*Colin Roberts*)

HST No. 43124 at New Street working the 10.25 Liverpool Lime Street to Plymouth, 11 May 1991. Driver Nick Power can be seen in the cab. (*Author*)

Lawley Street goods depot, Birmingham. (*Author's collection*)

another incendiary bomb came down a ventilation shaft and landed on the running plate. The driver stopped and the fireman shovelled it off. Fireman Archie Gunning recalled that on one occasion when he was in a Birmingham blitz, his driver sheltered under the engine, but expected him to remain on the footplate and maintain the fire and water. On 10 April 1941, bombs closed the Western Suburban Tunnels for eight days, so LMS trains were diverted between Birmingham and the south via Kidderminster.

A signalman at New Street was walking back to his box after filling his coal bucket, when he looked up to watch a dog fight between British and German planes. This distraction caused him to trip over a rail and, while lying across the line, he became aware of a train almost upon him. There was no time to stand and move away – the only escape from death was to lie down between the rails. Unfortunately, his coat became caught under the train and he was dragged along until it stopped. He was so seriously injured that he was off work for a year and when he did eventually return, could only carry out signalling duty at boxes with less intensive traffic.

A Bath crew, driver Ralph Holden and fireman Bob Ford, were at New Street Platform 6 working the Down Leicester Parcels. On the left, under a high wall, was a siding into the Market Hall and in it were two parcels vans which they had to pick up and place on the front of their train. The signal box was about 30 yards from them, across to the right. The signalman's own personal air raid shelter looked like a dalek – a dome-shaped iron affair with a door (illustrated on page 106). Fireman Ford said he would not have been anxious to use it and would have preferred to take refuge in the tunnel only a few yards away.

Ralph drew the parcels train forward into the tunnel before setting back to collect the vans. Bob and Ralph waited in the tunnel for ten minutes. Bob had made sure that the safety valves would not lift because it was almost a dismissal offence to blow off in New Street station as the Queen's Hotel, owned by the LMS, stood just above that wall by the Market Hall and a violent escape of steam would have disturbed sleeping guests.

Bob, standing on the ground to observe the disc signal being pulled off as steam and smoke in the tunnel made it invisible from the cab exclaimed, 'There's something wrong!' They knew German raiders were around because they could hear bombs exploding. Bob walked to the tunnel mouth, but could see no sign of the signalman in his box.

Eventually a shunter came along and said, 'There's a lot of trouble back there, they've dropped a bomb on the Market Hall. Those parcel vans are gone for a Burton.' 'Where's the bobby?' inquired Bob. 'Oh, he's in his shelter.' 'Well, fetch him out, as we're not able to go in the Market Hall now, we want to get out of Brum immediately.'

With the utmost difficulty, the shunter persuaded the scared signalman to leave his shelter, enter his box, pull the points, move the disc and allow them to set back on to their train. The shunter coupled up, the bobby pulled the signal off and almost immediately raced down the steps back to his shelter. Ralph opened the regulator and in due course reached home safely. New Street was hit by raiders five times between 1940 and 1942.

New Street station was renewed in the 1960s, the eight through and six bay platforms replaced by twelve new platforms. It was the first time that BR invited private developers to help pay for a project. The platforms were covered by a reinforced concrete raft 7½ acres in extent, supporting a shopping centre. It was known as '407 deck' from its height in feet above sea level. The provision of an escalator was another 'first' for BR. The platforms were complete and all overhead wiring in place by 11 October 1966, though because 300–400 diesel trains would still pass through daily a ventilation scheme was devised, which unfortunately left something to be desired. Following the King's Cross tragedy, New Street was designated as an underground station by the fire service and the safety rules in force on the London Underground applied.

From Birmingham New Street (42 miles 53 chains), the line rises at 1 in 77/80 through Suffolk Street Tunnel, 176 yards; Holliday Tunnel 307 yards; Canal Tunnel 225 yards; Granville Street Tunnel 81 yards and Bath Row Tunnel 210 yd to reach Five Ways (43 miles 18 chains), a passengers-only station which closed 2 October 1944, but remained as a ticket platform. Prior to rebuilding, New Street was one of the few major stations in the country without ticket barriers. The reason was a public right of way along the footbridge which served all the platforms. At the top of the 1 in 80 gradient was Church Road station (43 miles 52 chains) closed 1 January 1925, its platforms remaining for almost fifty years longer. Immediately beyond is the 107-yard-long Church Road Tunnel. Somerset Road (44 miles 27 chains) closed 28 July 1930.

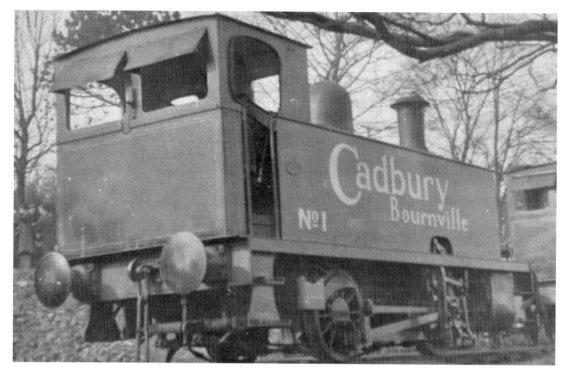

Cadbury's locomotive No. 1, seen preserved at Ashchurch, 26 June 1982. (*Revd Alan Newman*)

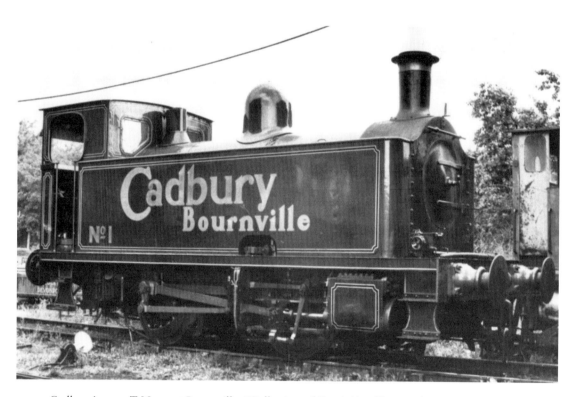

Cadbury's 0-4-0T No. 1 at Bournville. (*Collection of Revd Alan Newman*)

Two rakes of MR wagons each with a locomotive stand in Cadbury's works at Bournville, *c.* 1920. Notice the neatly folded sheets. (*Author's collection*)

The line undulated to University station (44 miles 73 chains) opened 8 May 1978 on a tight curve, and Selly Oak (45 miles 49 chains), which closed temporarily on 2 October 1944 and permanently in October 1950, later reopening on 8 May 1978. It lost its goods traffic on 2 November 1970. Bournville (46 miles 57 chains) is the station for Messrs Cadbury, though many of the workers did not need to use the railway regularly as the firm laid out a Garden City at Bournbrook. The railway was used for bringing in the raw ingredients and also coal, the firm owning eighty coal wagons by 1926. Additional incoming traffic was card, timber, tinplate, paper and strawboard. Cadbury's had a fleet of shunting engines, some built by Avonside and others by Dick, Kerr & Co. Its first diesel engine arrived in 1958, followed by three more in 1961 when regular steam working ceased. The railway closed on 8 May 1976. At the height of traffic, three trains of sixty four-wheeled vans left daily for the various Cadbury depots spread around the United Kingdom. South of Bournville and immediately before King's Norton (46 miles 58 chains) is the Lifford triangular junction where the line from Camp Hill joins. Between Lifford West Junction and King's Norton is the 60-yard-long Pershore Road Tunnel.

At King's Norton, a terrace of cottages built by the MR for its employees descends the hill. The station first opened in May 1849, had its platforms lengthened and additional buildings added in May 1885, then in 1925 was rebuilt as a four-road station, only the three-gabled building surviving. The station closed to goods traffic on 1 September 1964 and became unstaffed on 22 May 1967. After the morning rush hour, some suburban coach sets were stabled at King's Norton until needed for the afternoon peak. In the yard is the Carillion On Track Plant Depot.

King's Norton view Down, *c.* 1910. (*Courtesy W. H. Smith*)

4-4-0 No. 450 at King's Norton, 2 August 1921, with a Down train. (*W. L. Good*)

Northfield view Up, *c.* 1910. (*Author's collection*)

Northfield, *c.* 1905, showing the booking office enlarged 1902/03 and the new platform. (*Lens of Sutton*)

The 4 miles on a gradient of 1 in 301 up continue through Northfield (48 miles 10 chains), this section being quadrupled in April 1892 when the Up and Down platforms were replaced by an island serving the two central roads. The station had opened on 1 September 1870, closed to goods traffic on 6 July 1964 and became unstaffed on 22 May 1967. The section from Northfield to Halesowen Junction was quadrupled in the autumn of 1894. From Halesowen Junction the Great Western & Midland joint line left for Halesowen. Longbridge (49 miles 12 chains) closed in April 1849, but a works platform near its site was brought into use in 1916/17 and closed on 4 January 1960. A new station was opened on the site on 8 May 1978.

The 440-yard-long brick-lined Cofton Tunnel at the summit of the line was opened out between 10.15 p.m. on Saturday 26 January and 6.45 a.m. on Monday 28 January 1929 as part of the works required for quadrupling the section between Halesowen Junction and Barnt Green (51 miles 60 chains), junction of the line to Evesham. This section was a bottle-neck, which tried to accommodate over 170 trains daily. The tunnel partly collapsed on 11 May 1928, killing four workmen and injuring a further four.

The original scheme was to lay a temporary diversion on the east side of the tunnel about 3 feet above the springing level of the arch to carry traffic while the tunnel was demolished. Excavation over the tunnel began in March 1926, but geological faults were found, which demanded that the scheme be revised.

Cofton Tunnel: excavation around it almost completed and windows cut. Contractor's track. (*Author's collection*)

Cofton Tunnel: interior just prior to demolition. The timber is to protect the track and aid the removal of debris. (*Author's collection*)

Demolition of Cofton Tunnel, April 1928. (*Author's collection*)

Opening out Cofton Tunnel. (*Author's collection*)

The ground was unsuited for the proposed 1.5 to 1 slopes of the new cutting's sides. A large landslip occurred on the Up side and extra land could not be obtained, the Austin Motor Company requiring it for works extension. The only answer was the construction of a 28-foot-high wall, 440 yards in length, and the gradual removal of the tunnel as traffic allowed. June 1928 saw a further slip and it was decided to extend the concrete wall a further 9 yards – that is 9 yards longer than the length of the tunnel. With the wall complete, on Sunday 27 January 1929 it was decided to demolish the remainder of the tunnel with explosives, 2,000 tons of material being brought down. The Cofton scheme cost the LMS £250,000 and some of the 560,000 cubic yards of spoil was used to build up ground at the Austin works. Had the LMS authorities studied history, they could have spared themselves expense. Cofton Tunnel was not originally planned and was only started when serious slips in the slopes of an open cutting determined that a tunnel should be substituted.

At one time, platforms at Barnt Green were staggered, which was unusual for a junction station. The Up main platform was north of the junction and the Down main to the south, but in 1929 the Up platform for trains from Gloucester was moved south to a position opposite the Down to allow room for quadrupling. The station, its main building decorated in brick and stone, closed to goods on 6 July 1964 and became unstaffed on 22 May 1967.

Barnt Green, view Up, *c.* 1910, looking along the Evesham branch platform to the main line beyond. The boy below the footbridge has a tray of newspapers and sweets. (*Author's collection*)

The junction at Barnt Green viewed from the cab of No. 43124 working the 10.25 Liverpool Lime Street to Penzance, 11 May 1991. A DMU to Redditch stands on the left. (*Author*)

The main line platforms at Barnt Green, view Down, 5 February 1994. (*Author*)

The junction at Barnt Green, view Up, 5 February 1994. (*Author*)

No. 47828 passes Barnt Green with the 07.48 Swansea to York, 5 February 1994. (*Author*)

Barnt Green owes itself to the railway. Before the line came, it was just a sprinkling of cottages and even in the 1851 census the population was only forty-six. It was not until the 1880s that homes began to be built near the station and it developed into a commuter village with the station footbridge linking the two parts of the village. Unfortunately, electrification led to half of the bridge's attractive latticework being blanked off, but brought a £120,000 upgrade when the CrossCity platforms were raised and lengthened and the lighting improved. At one time, a weekly livestock sale was held on railway land below the embankment, but this moved to another site when the area was used for tipping spoil from Cofton Tunnel. As the Lickey Hills were a good place for Birmingham residents to get fresh air, on Saturdays and Sundays trains of nine corridor coaches, usually hauled by a 2-6-4T, offloaded its passengers, and very often an earlier train went back for a second load. They used the Redditch branch platform and if not returning for another load, backed out into one of the two loops.

One day, when a footplate crew was delayed at Barnt Green, they grew very cold on the footplate, while the signalman in his nice warm cabin laughed at them and failed to invite them to share his comfort. It was so cold in the cab that they took shelter by the smokebox where it was warmer. A month later, the signalman begged them for coal as his supply was running out – they gave him slack which they knew would not burn!

If the driver of a main line train saw a yellow signal in the Birmingham area, he proceeded very slowly before a station to try and avoid stopping at the platform, or else short-distance passengers would leap aboard and if a train stopped at a station, the Right Away had to be given by the guard.

Blackwell, view Down; the timber-built goods shed is to the right of the Up platform. (*Lens of Sutton*)

Fyffe's banana Vanfits pass Blackwell on an Up train, *c.* 1964. (*Richard Brown*)

Blackwell view Up, with the goods shed, almost hidden, immediately to the right of the station building. (*Lens of Sutton*)

Castle class 4-6-0 No. 7017 *George Jackson Churchward* at Blackwell, 16 March 1955, near the head of the incline. Notice how sharply the line drops away. (*W. Potter*)

The line falls at 1 in 291 for a mile to Blackwell (53 miles 15 chains), a brick building of typical Midland twin pavilion design with the rarer hipped roof rather than the more common gable pattern.

The Down refuge siding at Blackwell was converted to a goods loop on 21 June 1931 and extended on 23 July 1967. The station closed to goods on 3 February 1964 and was unstaffed from 13 December 1965, closing completely on 18 April 1966. Until the 1950s, special trains, generally hauled by a 2-6-4T, ran to Blackwell carrying visitors to the sanatorium. From Blackwell, the line descends the Lickey Incline to Bromsgrove (55 miles 31 chains).

The bridge carrying the road obliquely under the railway on the incline did not reach the standards imposed by the local authority so in July 1840, shortly before the line to Camp Hill was ready for opening, the BGR was forced to rebuild it. Herbert Spencer, as a young engineering assistant on 27 July, wrote,

I am engaged in superintending the pulling-down and re-erection of a large bridge under the inclined plane at Bromsgrove. It is to be completed within three weeks and four days from the commencement of the pulling-down, and rather more than one week has already passed. I have had to make out the drawings, estimate, etc, and to see to the details of the working during its progress ... I believe it will be done in time. The contract is between one and two thousand pounds.

The head of the incline viewed from the cab of No. 43124, 11 May 1991. The windscreen wipers can be seen in the lower right corner. (*Author*)

Type 3 English Electric D6922 gives rear assistance to 4-6-0 No. 6863 *Dolhywel Grange* up the Lickey Incline, 15 August 1964. (*Richard Brown*)

Class 9 2-10-0 No. 92137 descends the incline with a loaded coal train, 28 October 1963. (*Author*)

View up the incline, 16 April 1953, with a permanent way hut on the left. The Up road is of flat-bottomed rail, while the Down is bull-headed. The pipe supplying water to Bromsgrove shed is on the right. (*Dr A. J. G Dickens*)

A subsequent letter, written after the completion of the new bridge says,

You quite mistake as to the usual system of work on railways. The greater proportion of the work done at the bridge was by contract, and I had nothing to do with the men except to see that they did the company justice. All the timber work and fitting and fixing girders was, however, done by day-labour under my own instruction. Perhaps about half the cost of construction was in this case done by me and entirely after my own designs (Capt. Moorsom not interfering in any way); but this was an extreme case and the usual laws were broken through: day-working being strictly prohibited on this railway. The time allowed was so small that there was no possibility of designing fit girders and having them cast. Such girders as had been designed for other purposes, and could be obtained forthwith, were consequently used. These were, however, too short to span the width of the road obliquely; and the result was that a framework, partly of these girders and partly of strong timber baulks, had to be made.

View of the Up platform at Bromsgrove taken from the Down, 16 April 1963. (*Dr A. J. G. Dickens*)

Bromsgrove, view Up. Notice the recess in the platform by the point blades to give additional clearance. The incline commences below the bridge. (*Lens of Sutton*)

Bromsgrove, view Down. (*Lens of Sutton*)

Bromsgrove, view Up 4 June 1983, showing the new passenger platform. (*Author*)

Bromsgrove, 11 May 1991, viewed from the cab of No. 43015 *The Armada* working the 06.25 Plymouth to Newcastle. (*Author*)

2-4-0 No. 92 and a 4-4-0, probably No. 426, pass Bromsgrove with a Down express pre-1920. The locomotive works is to the right of No. 92's smokebox. (*Author's collection*)

4-6-0 No. 6985 *Parwick Hall* leaves a loop at Bromsgrove in 1964, while in the locomotive yard to the left stand a Class 8F 2-8-0 and a 84XX class 0-6-0PT. (*G. R. Dent*)

Peak Class Type 4 diesel-electric D66 approaches Bromsgrove with an Up express, 15 August 1964, while a 84XX class 0-6-0PT stands on the left. Notice the impresssive signal gantry. (*Richard Brown*)

At Bromsgrove, the Down platform was on a loop. All buildings were demolished in 1968, including the footbridge and Down platform. The three remaining trains that called of necessity used the Up platform, a portacabin forming the station building. A new Down platform was erected in April 1990 at a cost of £92,000, Hereford & Worcester County Council paying £60,000 and Bromsgrove District Council £10,000. A service was provided of nine each way, some on the Worcester to New Street service. Today, the station sees twenty-one trains each way offering a service of two an hour. Goods traffic ceased on 5 June 1967. East of the station was the locomotive works, later to become a wagon works, which closed 2 October 1964. At its peak, the works had handled 200 wagons weekly and employed 500 men, though by 1964 the workforce had dwindled to sixty-seven. During the autumn of 1966, construction commenced on a large oil and petrol storage depot south of Bromsgrove station.

When the railway works first opened, there was a general shortage of accommodation, many local residents taking in lodgers and making money from the situation. At Finstall Park, on the lower part of the incline, the arch of a large railway bridge was partly bricked up at the ends to provide makeshift accommodation.

Bromsgrove station was linked with the town by a horse bus seating ten inside and seven outside with the luggage. Commissioned by the Golden Cross Hotel, running costs were shared with the BGR. It was originally only reserved for first- and second-class passengers, though later on third-class passengers could travel for a 4d fare.

A less impressive view from the same location, 4 June 1983. (*Author*)

The oil terminal at Bromsgrove, 11 May 1991, viewed from the cab of a passing train. (*Author*)

Footplate view of Stoke Works from Class 9 2-10-0 No. 92156, 6 November 1963. (*W. F. Grainger*)

The driver of an Up train approaching Bromsgrove shuts down for the 80 mph restriction when two tall radio masts are in line. Maximum speed on the Bristol to Birmingham line is 100 mph.

The line south of Bromsgrove, falling at 1 in 283, was quadrupled to Stoke Works Junction, (57 miles 42 chains) on 10 February 1933, the Up slow being taken out of use 23 March 1969. At this junction, the line to Droitwich bears off to the west.

A certain amount of illicit barter took place on the railway. At Stoke Works, a girl arrived with a pram to beg some coal from an engine. The crew obliged and were given a large piece of bacon. They cooked some on a shovel in its fat. When they left the engine at Gloucester, they forgot to take away the remainder, so presumably the Bristol crew was able to enjoy it.

Droitwich Road (60 miles 19 chains), named merely Droitwich until 10 February 1852, closed to passengers on 1 October 1855, but the goods depot remained in use until 1 October 1952.

Dunhampstead (62 miles 11 chains) also closed to passengers on 1 October 1855 and ceased handling goods traffic on 1 October 1949. The station at Spetchley (66 miles 17 chains), was another which closed to passengers on 1 October 1855, its usefulness as a coach head for Worcester ceasing after the opening of the railway in 1850. Spetchley closed to goods traffic on 2 January 1961.

Droitwich Road, *c.* 1920. (*Author's collection*)

Jubilee class 4-6-0 No. 5612 *Jamaica* with an early pattern Stanier tender, passes Spetchley in 1948. (*John Stamp*)

Bridge carrying the Oxford to Worcester line over the Gloucester to Birmingham line, viewed from the cab of No. 43015 *The Armada,* working the 06.25 Plymouth to Newcastle, 11 May 1991. (*Author*)

Abbot's Wood Junction, 11 May 1991, viewed from the cab of No. 43015 *The Armada.* (*Author*)

The timber building at Wadborough, view Up. Notice the sleeper-built crossing in the foreground linking the platforms. The station is neatly kept and enhanced with boxes of flowers. (*Author's collection*)

North of Abbot's Wood Junction (68 miles 59 chains), the line passes under the Oxford, Worcester & Wolverhampton Railway, while the line from Worcester comes in at the junction. The MR had running powers to Worcester and its own goods depot in the city. Abbot's Wood Junction, an exchange station only, was yet another to be affected by closure on 1 October 1855.

One day, fireman Tommy Knight had a very large and hard lump of coal, which he was unable to split into a size small enough to fit into the firebox. As it was useless, at Abbot's Wood he kicked it off the footplate and even when it landed on the ground, it still failed to split, but went through a sleeper-built permanent way men's shed.

For many years, the 12½ miles between Stoke Works and Wadborough was one of the longest stretches in the country without a station. Wadborough station (69 miles 79 chains) closed its timber buildings to passengers on 4 January 1965 and had no goods sidings, but was served by Pirton Sidings just over half a mile to the south. Pirton (70 miles 50 chains) opened to passengers in November 1841 and closed to passengers three years later, the goods yard, renamed Pirton Sidings, remaining in use until 1 July 1963. Defford station (73 miles 39 chains), built in

BRITISH RAILWAYS BOARD

PUBLIC NOTICE

TRANSPORT ACT 1962

WITHDRAWAL OF RAILWAY PASSENGER SERVICES

The Western Region of British Railway hereby give notice, in accordance with Section 56(7) of the Transport Act 1962, that on and from Monday 11th November 1963 they propose to discontinue the local stopping passenger services between

BRISTOL (TEMPLE MEADS)—GLOUCESTER (EASTGATE)—WORCESTER (SHRUB HILL)
and from the following stations:

Fishponds.	Coaley
Staple Hill	Stonehouse (Bristol Rd.)
Mangotsfield	Haresfield
Yate	Bredon
Wickwar	Eckington
Charfield	Defford
Berkeley Road	Wadborough

It appears to the Board that the following alternative services will be available.

BY RAIL.
Bristol (Temple Meads), Gloucester (Eastgate), Cheltenham Spa (Lansdown), Ashchurch and Worcester (Shrub Hill) will be served by the through trains as at present which will continue to operate over the line. An alternative rail service is available between Gloucester (Central) and Cheltenham (St James). The 7.50 a.m. train Worcester (Shrub Hill) to Gloucester (Eastgate) and the 4.48 p.m. Gloucester (Eastgate) to Worcester (Shrub Hill) will run at amended times serving intermediately Cheltenham Spa (Lansdown) and Ashchurch.

It is proposed to arrange for the 11.25 a.m. Birmingham to Cardiff and the 5.20 p.m. Derby to Cardiff trains to call additionally at Ashchurch at approximately 12.20 p.m. and 7.20 p.m. respectively, weekdays only.

BY BUS

BRISTOL OMNIBUS COMPANY LTD.

Service No.	Route	Service No.	Route
26	Bristol—Gloucester	115	Gloucester—Sharpness
29	Bristol—Cheltenham	116	Gloucester—Dursley
29a	Bristol—Sharpness	117	Gloucester—Leonard Stanley
31	Bristol—Swindon	119	Gloucester—Stonehouse
32	Bristol—Cirencester	128	Bristol—Chippenham
49	Gloucester—Cheltenham	131	Bristol—Chipping Sodbury
49a	Gloucester—Cheltenham	147b	Downend—Chipping Sodbury
50	Gloucester—Evesham	164	Gloucester—Cheltenham
51	Gloucester—Stonehouse	319	Bristol—Dyrham
52	Gloucester—Frocester	400	Bristol—Stroud.
62	Cheltenham—Priors Park	461	Stroud—Dursley
62b	Cheltenham—Priors Park		Also the Bristol City Services.

BRISTOL OMNIBUS CO. LTD. AND STRATFORD-UPON-AVON BLUE MOTORS JOINT SERVICE
64a   Cheltenham—Evesham.

THE BIRMINGHAM AND MIDLAND MOTOR OMNIBUS CO. LTD.

X 72	Birmingham—Gloucester	381	Pershore—Tewkesbury
X 73	Birmingham—Cheltenham	335	Evesham—Worcester
X 74	Birmingham—Cheltenham	386	Worcester—Pershore
X 91	Leicester—Hereford	387	Worcester—Evesham.

BLUE COACH SERVICES

— Worcester—Pirton & High Green	— Worcester—Defford

OBJECTIONS
Any user of the rail service it is proposed to withdraw and any body representing such users desirous of objecting to the proposal may lodge objections within six weeks of Saturday, 10th August 1963. i.e., not later than Saturday, 21st September 1963, addressing any objection to the Secretary of the South Western Area Transport Users' Consultative Committee, Magnet House 32. Victoria Street, Bristol 1, if the objection relates to closures in the County of Gloucestershire, or to the Secretary of the West Midland Area Transport Users' Consultative Committee, 29, Smallbrook, Ringway, Birmingham 5, if it relates to closures in the county o Worcestershire.

NOTE.—If any objections are lodged within the period specified, the closure cannot be proceeded with until the Transport Users' Consultative Committee have reported to the Minister of Transport and the Minister has given his consent in accordance with section 56(8) of the Transport Act 1962.

Eth188

Public notice of the withdrawal of railway passenger services between Gloucester (Eastgate) and Worcester (Shrub Hill), published on 8 August 1963.

Defford view Up, *c.* 1905. A water crane can be seen on the far right, while another stands at the far end of the Up platform. (*Author's collection*)

domestic style as were many of the BGR stations, had water cranes and closed to goods on 1 July 1963 and to passengers on 4 January 1965. A rare feature of Defford station was that there were no doors from the main building to the platform. The station was inconveniently sited, as although the railway ran only about 200 yards from the village, the station was set three times this distance along a footpath. Pirton Sidings and Defford signal boxes both had contact with the nearby airfield, as when planes came in low, trains had to be stopped. The airfield was used for training paratroopers and also for developing the top-secret radar.

A quarter of a mile south of Defford station was the 83-yard-long, three-arch River Avon Viaduct. Moorsom's method of using iron caissons filled with concrete for the foundations of this bridge won him the Telford Medal of the Institution of Civil Engineers. It was the very first practical example of iron caissons being sunk to form a chamber which, when the water had been pumped out, was filled with concrete and masonry.

The work consisted of three cast-iron segmented arches, each of 73-foot span, supported on two lines of iron columns resting on caissons filled with concrete. When rebuilt in 1931, single track working was instituted while the Down spans and then the Up spans were being replaced, a special signal box, 'Avon Bridge', being brought into use for the purpose. The 1931 bridge was a modernised version of the old, the plate girders being relieved by a delicate iron fence at the top. On Sundays, fishermen's trains ran from Birmingham to Defford and Eckington.

The bridge at Defford across the River Avon, 1839. Each 58-foot span is 28 feet above the water. (*Lithograph by Clerk & Co.*)

No. 50026 *Indomitable,* heading the 11.33 Manchester Piccadilly to Plymouth, crosses Defford Bridge, 4 June 1983. (*Author*)

Bredon, view Up, *c.* 1910, showing the house and running-in board. (*Author's collection*)

Bredon, view Down, *c.* 1963. (*Lens of Sutton*)

Bredon, view Up. There are attractive flowerbeds on both platforms. (*Lens of Sutton*)

The closure dates of Eckington (74 miles 47 chains) and Bredon (77 miles 25 chains) stations are the same as Defford. Although railway boundaries almost invariably follow the edge of a cutting, or the foot of an embankment, near Eckington the former owner of the land when selling it in 1838 reserved all rights on the slopes, so the fence is placed at the top of the embankment. It is said that one West Country Pacific working a special train reached 104 mph through Bredon – the limit on that stretch of line being 75 mph due to the relatively short distance between the distant and home signals. Ashchurch (79 miles 37 chains) was a junction station with two platforms for the main line, one for the Tewkesbury branch leaving to the west and one for the Evesham branch to the east. The alternative line to Birmingham via Evesham, avoiding the Lickey Incline but with miles of single track, was 5 miles 16 chains longer.

At the Up end of Ashchurch station, the Tewkesbury to Evesham line crossed the Birmingham to Gloucester track on the level, this being taken out of use on 5 May 1957. The station closed to goods on 1 January 1964, was unstaffed on 14 September 1970 and closed completely on 15 November 1971. The main station building was on the Up side of the main line, its most impressive features being the large bay window facing south and the ridge and furrow glass canopy. No canopy was provided for the Tewkesbury and Evesham passengers – perhaps the MR assumed they were more used to the elements than city folk using the main line.

Ashchurch, *c.* 1905, with the Tewkesbury branch left, the line to Birmingham straight ahead and the Evesham branch right. The 0-6-0 has outside frames. Notice the lamp pots in the coach roof. (*Author's collection*)

Ashchurch view Up from a similar viewpoint, 4 June 1983. The old station has closed and a new one yet to be opened. (*Author*)

Ashchurch view Down, 1954, to the road overbridge from which the two previous views were taken. Ashchurch Level Crossing signal box, closed 27 July 1958, is on the far left. (*Dr A .J. G. Dickens*)

Jubilee class 4-6-0 No. 45602 *British Honduras* approaches the level crossing at Ashchurch with the 12.30 p.m. York to Bristol Temple Meads, 9 July 1955. (*Hugh Ballantyne*)

The Midland Railway water tower near the north end of Ashchurch Up platform, still standing on 11 September 2012. (*Author*)

The Dowty Hydraulic Units Ltd's testing site for wagon buffing and draw gear, *c.* 1958. Each ramp has a 1 in 3.7 gradient offering speeds up to 25 mph. The control tower is nearby. A test curve is to the left. The Tewkesbury branch is in the background. (*Author's collection*)

4-6-0 No. 7808 *Cookham Manor*, preserved at Ashchurch in 1968. (*W. H. Harbor*)

DMU No. 150129 at Ashchurch with the 17.06 Worcester to Westbury, 11 September 2012. (*Author*)

ERO.19857

LONDON MIDLAND AND SCOTTISH RAILWAY COMPANY.

FROM CHIEF OPERATING MANAGER'S OFFICE   Office.   S.O.

Derby.

12 - 3 1934

Dear Sir,

    I am in receipt of your letter of the 10th inst.

    Please go to Ashchurch on March 19th

prepared for work, and report yourself to the Station Master.

Mr._____ on arrival.

    I enclose a free ticket for your journey.

        Yours faithfully,

        For C. R. BYROM.

Mr. G. R. T. Harrison

A duplicated form sent from the Chief Operating Manager's Office, Derby, 12 March 1934, offering a post at Ashchurch to G. R. T. Harrison.

The station's refreshment room doubled as the local pub, well patronised by soldiers based at the large camp a short distance along the Evesham branch. Two signal boxes, Ashchurch Junction and Level Crossing, closed on 27 July 1958 and were replaced by Ashchurch signal box. Probably a good idea at the time, history proved it a rather futile move as the new box was superseded on 16 February 1969 by the power box at Gloucester. The goods yard south of the passenger station was busy handling a variety of items. It was estimated that early in the twentieth century over a 100 employees worked on the railway at Ashchurch at the passenger station, goods yards, provender store and signal boxes. The former brick-built MR provender store was taken over by Dowty Engineering. The Dowty Railway Preservation Society was formed in 1962 and for the next twenty years, kept narrow and standard gauge stock on a nearby site. The provender store no longer stands. Until pressure on the site forced them out in the early 1980s, the Dowty Railway Preservation Society had a centre at Ashchurch. War Department sidings were opened on the Evesham branch at Ashchurch. Although the branch closed on 9 September 1963, these sidings remain open. During the Second World War, these siding were worked by an ex-LNWR 2-4-2T on loan to the WD.

As a result of lobbying, particularly from Tewkesbury, on 30 May 1997 a new station, Ashchurch for Tewkesbury, was opened on the old site. The two concrete

Cleeve, view Down, 1884, showing the old timber bridge. (*Author's collection*)

Cleeve, view Up, showing the construction of its successor. (*Author's collection*)

Cleeve, view Down, 26 July 1953. The replacement signal box, right, opened on 19 November 1944 and closed 17 February 1969. Notice the rare MR cast-iron urinal midway between the station building and the vans. (*Author's collection*)

Star class 4-6-0 No. 4052 *Princess Beatrice* races through Cleeve, 25 September 1949, with a Wolverhampton to Penzance Sunday diversion. (*C. H. A. Townley*)

platforms are connected by a long-ramped, open, metal footbridge. Metal and glass bus stop-type shelters are on both platforms.

Although most drivers were thoroughly responsible, one or two had a weakness and some working stopping trains between Gloucester and Birmingham got out at each station which had a pub nearby, had a drink and by the end of their turn were too drunk to drive, the engine both driven and fired by the fireman. Ashchurch had a pub on the platform, while Bredon, Eckington, Defford and Dunhampstead all had pubs close to the station.

From Ashchurch the line climbs almost continuously at 1 in 295–322 to Cheltenham. Cleeve station (82 miles 74 chains) opened on 14 February 1843, just under three years after the line opened. A simple station, it had a small main building on the Down platform and a shelter on the Up. Goods facilities consisted of a shed served by a loop on the Down side. Cleeve closed to passengers on 20 February 1950 and to goods on 4 April 1960. A station called Swindon (84 miles 23 chains) – the name must have caused confusion to some passengers – opened on 26 May 1842 and closed on 1 October 1844.

At Cheltenham, the High Level sidings west of the Up line and the line leading to and from them was on a heavy gradient; in the interest of safety, inwards traffic was required to be taken in front of the engine in rakes not exceeding ten 10-ton, or twelve 8-ton wagons. Outwards traffic had to be moved behind the engine and not less than one wagon brake applied for every three loaded, or four empty wagons.

Cheltenham High Street Halt (85 miles 68 chains) passenger station opened 1 September 1862, immediately south of Tewkesbury Road. Originally named Cheltenham Tewkesbury Road Bridge, it was renamed 1 October 1862. It closed on 1 July 1910. Extensive sidings at High Street were lifted in 1966. Alston Sidings, north of Cheltenham Lansdown, still remain and are used by Arriva Trains Wales and First Great Western.

South-east of the station was the Gloucester Road Gasworks, served first by the Gloucester & Cheltenham tramroad and from about 1850 by road from the MR sidings. From April 1897, a half-mile-long standard gauge line was built from the MR yard to an elevated tipping dock at the gasworks. Shunting on this line was carried out by horses and MR locomotives until 1920 when the Cheltenham & District Gas Company bought its own locomotive. In September 1964 ex-Port of Bristol 0-6-0ST No. S10 *Hallen* was purchased to replace 0-4-0ST Peckett Works No. 1835, which had failed. In the interim a steam crane had been used for shunting, but the PBA engine proved clumsy in a different way and was taken away for scrap in November 1967. The works used approximately 30,000 tons of coal in 1897, and this figure increased to 36,473 tons in 1914 and about 50,000 tons in the 1950s. Points on the MSWJR engine shed line giving communication with the gasworks were controlled by tablet which was kept by the gasworks foreman, the padlock key being kept in the MR yard foreman's office. The introduction of North Sea gas in 1969 caused the works to become redundant and in 1976 a coal concentration depot took part of the gasworks' sidings site. Now closed, this coal depot was worked by two diesel-hydraulic shunting engines.

Cheltenham Gasworks Peckett 0-4-0ST Works No. 1835 of 1934, seen here on 5 April 1962. It wears a livery of dark green, lined with yellow and black. (*Hugh Ballantyne*)

Two-car DMU C976 stabled in Alston Sidings, 11 May 1991, viewed from cab of an Up HST – the windscreen wipers appear at the foot of the picture. (*Author*)

MR 0-6-0 No. 413 heads a Down train at Cheltenham. (*Author's collection*)

2-4-0 No. 20216 at Cheltenham, 16 April 1949. Built at Derby in 1879, it was withdrawn in November 1949. To the left of the smokebox can be seen a water crane and the 'devil' lit in cold weather to prevent freezing. (*T. G. Wassell*)

Class 9 2-10-0 No. 92151 (2E, Saltley), heads a Down coal train through Cheltenham, 1964. (*W. F. Grainger*)

Cheltenham Lansdown, view Up, *c.* 1963. The platforms are covered with typical MR ridge and furrow canopies. (*Lens of Sutton*)

Cheltenham Lansdown (86 miles 56 chains) is a fine building in classical style. Gordon Biddle in *Victorian Stations* claims it was adapted from an existing mansion set 1¼ miles from the town and fitting the stipulation that the station should be at a 'respectable distance' from the town centre. Samuel W. Dawkes, a Cheltenham architect who designed fine churches in the town and elsewhere, as well as Friern Hospital in north London, was responsible for adding to the stucco frontage with a shallow central pediment and Palladian windows, the railway addition of a deep nine-bay Doric colonnade with plain entablature. Unfortunately, BR removed the colonnade in 1961. Its roof was a large tank for providing rainwater for locomotive use. Up and Down main line platforms, at first within a train shed supported by stanchions so close to the platform edge that open carriage doors only just cleared them, were later covered by typical MR ridge and furrow awnings. Although lengthened in 1961, the station is largely still in its 1840 condition.

A two-platform bay, referred to as the Horse Box, or Ladies' College bay due to its alternative uses, was brought into use in January 1900 to cope with extra traffic brought by the Midland & South Western Junction Railway (MSWJR), which had opened to Cheltenham on 1 August 1891. MSWJR passenger trains worked to and from Lansdown, using the through platforms as well as the bay, and running powers extended to High Street. Coaching stock was stored immediately north of Lansdown station and two MSWJR parcels vans kept in the dock at Lansdown. The goods sidings, eight for exchange and two joint, were at High Street. The MSWJR engine shed alongside the exchange sidings closed 28 December 1935. A notice by the tea room at Lansdown read: 'Change here for Swindon, Marlborough, Andover, Portsmouth, Southampton, Cherbourg and France.'

Around 1940, the YMCA provided temporary sleeping accommodation at Cheltenham for servicemen. (*Author's collection*)

A 4-2-2 and a 2-4-0 head an Up express at Cheltenham in the early 1900s. (*Author's collection*)

No. 43172 calls at Cheltenham with the 07.26 Derby to Penzance, 22 May 1982. (*Author*)

Midland & South Western Junction Railway 4-4-4T No. 18 at Cheltenham Lansdown with a Down express. (*Author's collection*)

SR U class 2-6-0 No. 31613 at Cheltenham, 23 August 1958, with a train of ex-GWR coaches to Andover. (*C. H. A. Townley*)

Cheltenham Lansdown seen from the cab of Class 8F 2-8-0 No. 48388 in March 1963. The bay platform, used by some MSWJR trains, is on the right. (*W. F. Grainger*)

Following closure of the MSWJR on 9 September 1961, the bay was lifted on 10 October 1965 and the Down platform extended, the Up platform having been lengthened the previous year when the short spur sidings at the southern end were lifted. The BGR was responsible for building Queen's Road, a splendid half-mile-long approach to the station. The station's original name of Cheltenham (Queen's Road, Lansdown) was changed to Cheltenham Spa (Lansdown) on 1 February 1925. Many horse boxes were in evidence on race days and nannies brought young children to see the animals being unloaded and loaded. The water columns at Cheltenham were marked with a broad red band about halfway up. This was because it was mains water, therefore expensive and only to be taken in an emergency. On summer Saturdays, an inspector was stationed there to check that this regulation was complied with.

At Lansdown Junction (86 miles 71 chains) the line from Honeybourne and Cheltenham St James' came in, while the line to Banbury diverged, this branch closing on 15 October 1962. Beyond was Hatherley Junction (87 miles 47 chains) forming the third side of the triangle and this curve closed in 1956. Track changes at Lansdown Junction in 1958 robbed ex-Midland & South Western Junction

Class 8F 2-8-0 No. 48133 approaches Hatherley Junction, 9 November 1963. (*W. F. Grainger*)

Railway trains of the route into Lansdown station, and from 3 November the solitary surviving through train was diverted to Cheltenham St James. This meant that the MSWJR was no longer a through route and as local traffic was insufficient to keep the line alive, it closed 9 September 1961.

From Cheltenham, the main line falls at 1 in 304–368 towards Gloucester. The first station at Churchdown (89 miles 68 chains) opened on 9 August 1842 and closed on 27 September the same year. The second station, operated jointly by the MR and GWR, opened on 2 February 1874. The main building, of brick, stood on the Down side. For many years, attractive station gardens were a feature. When the line through the station was quadrupled in July 1942, the additional goods-only tracks were laid on the outside edges of the two platforms, making them islands. The lines to Hatherley Junction were quadrupled on 9 August 1942 and Churchdown station had its platforms widened in March 1944 so that they could be used by passenger trains. The station closed to passengers on 2 November 1964 and the line reverted to double track two years later. The GWR carried out maintenance from Lansdown Junction to a board 15 chains south of Churchdown station, the MR carrying out maintenance from this board to Gloucester.

Churchdown station, view Down, *c.* 1920. (*Author's collection*)

An Up train passes through Churchdown, *c.* 1910. (*Author's collection*)

Churchdown, view Up, 16 April 1953, following quadrupling. The GWR signal box opened on 28 June 1942. (*Dr A. J. G. Dickens*)

72XX class 2-8-2T No. 7204 at Churchdown in 1938 before quadrupling of the line during the Second World War. (*W. Vaughan-Jenkins*)

In 1942, a borrow pit has been excavated on the right to provide material for widening the embankment for quadrupling. (*Author's collection*)

Churchdown 1942, view Down: two new side spans extend the existing bridge over the quadrupling. (*Author's collection*)

Class 8F 2-8-0 No. 48388 on the quadrupled track near Churchdown, March 1964. (*W. F. Grainger*)

Class 8F 2-8-0 No. 48133 passes a sister engine near Churchdown, 9 November 1963. (*W. F. Grainger*)

Class 8F 2-8-0 No. 48133 passes Class 9 2-10-0 No. 92151 near Churchdown, 9 November 1963. (*W. F. Grainger*)

On 6 November 1963 Class 9 2-10-0 No. 92156 meets a three-car DMU near Churchdown. (*W. F. Grainger*)

Class 8F 2-8-0 No. 48388 at Engine Shed Junction, Gloucester, March 1964. To the right is a three-car Swindon Cross-Country DMU. The ex-LMS Barnwood engine shed was to the left and behind the photographer. (*W. F. Grainger*)

At Engine Shed Junction (92 miles 23 chains), the Gloucester Avoiding Line bears off. Engine Shed Junction, was renamed Barnwood Junction on 26 May 1968 the name no longer being appropriate as the depot had closed. Nearby was Barnwood locomotive shed and Barnwood Yard with twenty-one roads, with Tramway Junction situated at its far end. Here the BGR crossed both Horton Road and the Gloucester & Cheltenham tramroad at right angles on the level, the BGR installing gates and building a lodge on the south side for the gatekeeper. The jointly owned four-road (two standard and two broad gauge) transfer shed measured 150 feet by 60 feet and was capable of holding at least twenty wagons of each gauge.

The BGR's terminal station (93 miles 28 chains) at Gloucester measured approximately 240 feet by 75 feet and had two platform roads – arrival and departure – and two central carriage sidings, all covered by a train shed. The four roads were connected at the west end by turntables.It was situated immediately south of the GWR and Bristol & Gloucester station. When the Bristol & Gloucester Railway was taken over by the MR and became standard gauge, trains from Bristol used the BGR station. The BGR/MR goods depot was sited further south. The junction with the line to Bristol was just outside the station at Passenger Junction signal box. To obviate the awkward and time-consuming reversal in or out, on 12 April 1896 a new MR station opened (93 miles 12 chains). The buildings were in the domestic revival style, lavishly endowed with pedimented ballustrading.

Gloucester Eastgate, view Up, *c.* 1905: 1853 class 4-2-2 No. 94 stands on the right. Both engines have shining buffers. (*Author's collection*)

Gloucester view Up, June 1910; notice the ridge-and-furrow roof and the gas lamps. A 4-2-2 heads a Down express. (*Author's collection*)

Cab view from a similar location fifty years later: notice that the signals have been changed from lower to upper quadrant. An ex-GWR 0-6-0PT stands on the right. (*W. F. Grainger*)

An LMS 0-6-0 leaves Gloucester in the Up direction, *c.* 1935. (*M. J. Tozer*)

4-4-0 No. 632 waits at Gloucester beside a Southern Railway cattle wagon, *c.* 1935. (*M. J. Tozer*)

Gloucester Eastgate, 17 August 1963: view, taken from the cab of BR Standard Class 5 4-6-0 No. 73021, of Jubilee class 4-6-0 No. 45658 *Keyes* arriving with a Down express. Gloucester Passenger Station signal box can be seen between the two locomotives with a GWR water tank beyond. Spotters are on the right, while on the far right is the ex-GWR Horton Road shed closed to steam in December 1965. (*W. F. Grainger*)

Driver S. Stone of Barrow Road shed stands by his BR Standard Class 5 4-6-0 No. 73021, which has worked a train from Bristol. Note the substatial water column and the 'devil' beside it, lit in cold weather to prevent freezing. The gas lamp has been extended in height. (*W. F. Grainger*)

No. 73021 on the turntable at Gloucester Eastgate ready for the return journey, 17 August 1963. (*W. F. Grainger*)

A Peak class diesel-electric heads a Down express at Gloucester Eastgate, *c.* 1966. (*Derrick Payne*)

Class oF o-4-oT No. 41535, Gloucester Docks shunter, at Eastgate, 16 May 1959. WR Horton Road shed is in the right background. (*R. E. Toop*)

Class oF 0-4-0T No. 41535 (85B, Gloucester) shunting on the Docks branch, 2 November 1962. (*Revd Alan Newman*)

A typical MR ridge and furrow roof was supported by rolled steel beams set on cast-iron columns. The platforms, set on a sharp curve, were: No. 2 Up Through, No. 1 Up Bay, while on the Down side was an island having platform Nos 3 and 4. This became 'closed' for ticket purposes on 23 November 1914, the station being entirely 'closed' from 17 April 1919. A consequent result of this was that the long footbridge linking the MR and GWR stations could only be used by ticket holders. This led to criticism as inhabitants on the north side of Gloucester were unable to use the bridge to reach the MR station, or those on the south side to reach the GWR station, some citizens complaining that this was unjust treatment as the building of the bridge had been a compromise to avoid the cost of constructing a joint station. In order to make crossing it easier, staff kept communal bicycles at each end of the 190-yard-long bridge.

On 17 September 1951, British Railways named the ex-MR station 'Eastgate' to differentiate it from the former GWR station, which became 'Central'. Eastgate was combined with Central station as just 'Gloucester' on 26 May 1968, closed on 1 December 1975 when the former Central station was officially reopened after modernisation at a cost of £250,000. Eastgate had closed to goods on 1 August 1967. The High Orchard branch closed on 1 October 1971.

Chapter Three

Locomotives

In 1838, Edward Bury, locomotive superintendent of the London & Birmingham Railway, was engaged by the BGR as locomotive agent and advisor. He ordered four engines from George Forrester & Co. at £1,660 apiece, but for immediate constructional needs, purchased Stephenson 0-4-0 *Planet* from the Leicester & Swannington Railway and a 0-4-2 from the London & Southampton Railway. They were renamed *Leicester* and *Southampton* respectively. The first two Forrester engines arrived in November 1838 and worked on building the southern section of the line, while the remaining engines were promised in mid-1839.

The directors had intended to work the Lickey Incline with a stationary engine and Bury set to work on its design. Captain W. S. Moorsom, the company's engineer, had other ideas and intended to work the incline with locomotives and so prove his critics Brunel, Bury and Stephenson wrong.

Moorsom, impressed with the information in the catalogue regarding the Norris engine *George Washington* tackling the 1 in 14 gradient on the Portsmouth & Roanoke Railway in the United States of America, with the Lickey Incline in mind, decided to order some of these machines for use on the BGR. P. C. Dewhurst, in a paper read to the Institute of Civil Engineers at London on 15 October 1947, claimed that Moorsom would have been too busy to have actually observed the locomotive and merely learned of it through a circular letter, which seemed to provide a providential solution to the difficulties of working the steep gradient on his line. Commentators have stated that British locomotive builders could have supplied suitable engines to work the gradient and that 0-6-0s would have been a far better wheel arrangement than the 4-2-0 of the Norris.

Moorsom stated, 'it was not until two celebrated makers in England had refused to take an order that negotiations were set on foot with Mr Norris.' In February 1838, Moorsom received instructions from his directors to have three engines ready by the following January. Matters seem to have hung fire, for it was not until 10 October that he reported tenders from sixteen builders and that, 'Mr Norris of Philadelphia offers to supply an assistant engine for working up the inclined plane'. The overtures from other manufacturers were not for incline locomotives and the four engines ordered from Forrester at £1,660 each were for the southern section of line. Norris offered a locomotive (Class A Extra) at £1,750 without tender, on condition that, if it made the agreed performance in the

Transhipment in 1846 from a standard gauge wagon, left, to a broad gauge wagon at Gloucester. (*Courtesy: Illustrated London News*)

USA under judges appointed by the BGR, or ran in England for a month under test conditions, the BGR would purchase it and order another ten in the ensuing eighteen months.

Within a month, William Gwynne, Norris's European representative, persuaded the BGR to also test a smaller (Class B) engine costing £1,545 with tender. The larger engine was specified as being able to haul a load of 75 tons, including engine and tender, up the 2 mile 66 yd gradient at 10–15 mph, while the smaller was to haul 100 tons, including engine and tender, at 20 mph over the remainder of the line, subject to a ruling gradient of 1 in 300.

As the BGR was incomplete when *England,* a Class B engine, arrived in March 1839, it was tested on the Grand Junction Railway and found not to comply with the stipulated performance. Despite this failure, Gwynne persuaded BGR directors to buy *England,* but at the same time they insisted that the construction for the other six light Class B engines be rescinded and as regards the three heavy Class A Extras construction confirmed and carried out. The BGR directors were unaware that Norris had yet to design a Class A Extra and had ordered Gwynne to use delaying tactics in order to leave too little time for the BGR directors to change their minds and order from a British builder.

Undaunted, the silver-tongued Norris salesman set to work and the following week the BGR agreed to take six Class B engines at £1,525 each. As the Lickey Incline was still unfinished, Class A *Victoria* was tested on the 1 in 27/30 of the Bolton & Leigh Railway, but success was difficult to determine as Moorsom reported, 'the wretched state of the Bolton railway renders it impossible without the utmost danger to attempt to comply literally with the terms of the agreement'. It was only possible to discover that it could haul 39½ tons, including its own weight, up the bank at 13 mph. *Victoria* was purchased for £1,200 without tender. The BGR also ordered three Class B engines from B. Hick & Son, six from Nasmyth, Gaskell & Co., the latter costing only £1,050 each.

Philadelphia, a Class A Extra, was delivered at the end of May 1840, and in June and July tested on a hurriedly prepared stretch of track on the Lickey Incline, just under a mile in length and at a gradient of 1 in 37.7. It had a sand box and water tub for wetting the rails to improve adhesion and succeeded in taking up 75 tons at 10 mph and 55 tons at 15 mph. On 23 August 1841, a comparative trial was run with Bury No. 65 from the London & Birmingham Railway. The Norris proved superior when coping with the heavier loads, the following results being obtained:

Load

Wagons	Carriages	Passengers	Weight	Speed of No. 65	Speed of Philadelpbia
3	1	15	24 tons 12 cwt	8.7 mph	15.1 mph
2	1	15	17 tons 18 cwt	13.9 mph	16.4 mph
1	1	15	11 tons 4 cwt	21 mph	17.4 mph
0	1	15	4 tons 10 cwt	24.6 mph	21.1 mph

Compared with British locomotives, the Norris engines were roughly built, this leading David Joy to note, 'The little thing could pull, but she was odd, plenty of cast iron in her, even the crosshead pins were cast iron.' Although they coped adequately on lightly laid American tracks, several of the Norris engines broke their chilled cast iron bogie wheels on the rigid BGR road, but there is no record of the English-built Norris type breaking their cast-iron bogie wheels. In the *Railway Magazine* for January 1909 Herbert T. Walker wrote that the working pressure of a Norris was supposed to be 62 lb/sq. inch, but critics claimed that the actual pressure was over 100 lb, which accounted for their smart getaway. *The Railway Times* of 28 September 1840 complained that two Norris engines were required to haul four to five coaches up the Lickey Incline.

The English engines were of far better finish and more accurate workmanship than those from the USA. In September 1840, almost all the Norris engines were reported as out of service owing to their fireboxes being of iron instead of the copper used in British locomotives. Burning wood in the USA the iron fireboxes and copper boiler tubes would last a reasonable time, but with the English use of coke, the fireboxes soon burnt through and the coke dust and cinders abraded the tubes. *Gloucester* had only run about 600 miles when her firebox needed replacing. The Haigh Foundry Co. supplied Class A engines with copper boxes at £115 each and Class B at £130. At the same time, their iron boiler tubes were replaced with those made from brass, at considerable expense. The purchase of the Norris engines was particularly hurtful for Bury. Between 1831 and 1837 he had exported twenty locomotives to the States, Norris had pirated his design and adapted it to suit American railroads.

The locomotive superintendent, William Creuze, was killed in April 1841 when *Boston* blew a plug on the Lickey Incline. He was replaced on 2 July 1841 by James Edward McConnell. He inherited thirty engines, of which only twelve were in a satisfactory running condition. In October 1841, he decided that engines should be changed over at Bromsgrove, thus giving him a chance to keep a close eye on the engines. Class B engines worked in the Birmingham Division and Class A in the Gloucester Division, mails being the exception. One pilot engine was to be kept at Gloucester, a bank engine at Camp Hill and two spare engines at Bromsgrove in addition to the pilot. McConnell gained a poor impression of the Norris engines, finding that although they performed reasonably when hauling light loads over lightly laid tracks, they were not sufficiently robust for general use over the BGR.

In February 1842, *Philadelphia* was converted to a saddle tank engine. This adaptation had the advantage of giving the engine additional adhesion weight from the water tanks and coal bunker, as well as abolishing the weight of the tender to be hauled; it also reduced coke consumption from seventeen to thirteen bags daily. It also meant that it ran no unproductive mileage. Alone it hauled trains up and down the incline, engine changing occurring at the head or foot of the incline. In May, two Class A Extras were bought for £1,000 each and may have been tank engines like *Philadelphia*. Three Class A Extras were kept at Bromsgrove for banking, but one often sufficed, being kept in steam for sixteen hours daily, but only making eight trips.

Due to the company's poor financial situation, in April 1842 drivers' pay was reduced from 7s to 6s for a twelve hour day and firemen's remuneration dropped from 6s to 5s, but footplate crews of mail trains only suffered a cut of 6d. Not surprisingly, drivers and firemen gave a fortnight's notice, so McConnell had to find fresh crews. Six fitters from Bromsgrove works volunteered and McConnell and his sister gave them a course in footplate work. During May, most of the men relented and accepted the directors' new terms. McConnell used a scheme for paying a premium for coke saving to bolster the enginemen's earnings to approximately the previous level. The company's coke bill fell from £3,170 in December 1842 to £2,197 in June 1843.

F. S. Williams in *The Midland Railway* states that the last use of a Norris engine was on the Tewkesbury branch. This would have been either *Philadelphia* or *Boston,* both having been rebuilt as saddle tanks and both withdrawn and broken up in June 1856.

When McConnell gave evidence before the Gauge Commission, he said that one of the Stothert, Slaughter & Co.'s largest goods engines, assisted by a pilot up the 1 in 55 incline out of Bristol, hauled a gross load of 235 tons and covered the 37½ miles to Gloucester in 4 hours 13 minutes, including four stops. At Gloucester, the freight was transhipped into standard gauge wagons and they left with a load of 254 tons. McConnell rode on the engine and the 51 miles from Gloucester to

Camp Hill station was covered in 3 hours 55 minutes, with six stops and banking up the Lickey Incline. This gave respective average speeds of 8¾ mph on the broad gauge and 13 mph on the standard and does not prove anything conclusive, except that it shows McConnell made a good run on the standard gauge.

In June 1845, No. 38 *Great Britain* was completed at the BGR's locomotive works at Bromsgrove. An 0-6-0ST designed by McConnell, it was the most powerful engine in the country and built specifically to assist trains up the Lickey Incline. It could handle a load of 135 tons and maintain a speed of 8–10 mph up the bank. Officially recorded rebuilt as 0-6-0WT No. 221 in December 1863, it was a sister to No. 223 of the previous year. The two were withdrawn in 1901 and 1928 respectively. In February 1847, McConnell left to take charge of the LNWR works at Wolverton, Matthew Kirtley of the MR taking over the Birmingham & Bristol's locomotive department.

Subsequent bankers were either standard engines, or standard engines slightly modified, in all cases being 0-6-0s, either tender or tank. January 1920 saw the appearance of No. 2290, Sir Henry Fowler's four cylinder 0-10-0 *Big Bertha*, by

An LMS signalman in an ARP (Air Raid Precaution) steel shelter. (*Author's collection*)

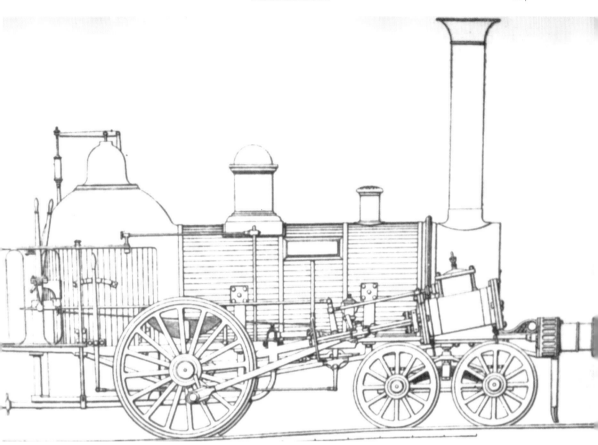

A Norris design 4-2-0 built by Benjamin Hick, Bolton. (*Author's collection*)

far the largest machine built by the MR and, for many years, the sole decapod working in Britain. Specially designed for banking, it was modified throughout the years.

After being placed in traffic making its trial trip on 1 January 1920, in 1922 an electric light was fitted to ensure gentle buffering up in the darkness, while to give better visibility towards the rear, the upper part of the tender was cut away. To comply with blackout restrictions during the Second World War, the power of the headlight was severely reduced by the use of black paint. She was maintained on a priority basis at Derby, visiting the works approximately annually. The main reason for *Big Bertha* being condemned in May 1956 was the failure of the dummy crank axle, (it was cranked to give clearance to the inside connecting rods which drove on to the centre coupled axle), together with the fact that her two boilers were becoming uneconomic to repair. When withdrawn in 1956 after covering 838,856 miles, nearly all on the Lickey Incline, she made her last trip on 6 May. Initially nicknamed 'Big Emma', she soon became known as *Big Bertha*, the name of a German rail-mounted super gun. *Big Bertha*'s electric headlight was fitted to BR Class 9F 2-10-0 No. 92079, which remained at Bromsgrove until October 1963.

F. R. M. Lawrence, in the *Railway Magazine* of July 1940, said that on a series of runs with eight-coach trains, after a dead stand at Bromsgrove, 15–16 mph was attained with No. 2290 at the rear, and a Black Five on the front, but with a Jubilee at the head and a Class 3F 0-6-0T banking, speeds were 21½–23 mph; with a 4-4-0 Compound and 0-6-0T speeds were 19–20 mph.

A reader explained in the October 1940 issue that owing to the desire to keep *Big Bertha*'s four cylinders in line, it was necessary to raise the middle cylinders considerably in order to clear the first and second axles, to enable all cylinders to drive the middle axle. The second coupled axle had to be cranked in order to clear the inside connecting rods. This meant that the height of these cylinders, of which the covers only just cleared the bottom of the smokebox, made it impossible to fit piston valves above the cylinder barrels, so that the unusual arrangement of crossing the inside cylinder ports had to be resorted to. With the short lap valve gear fitted, this resulted in excessive clearance volume and premature release, making working less efficient. In June 1941, when *Big Bertha* was being overhauled at Derby, several temporary banking engines were brought in from Worcester shed, including LNER J39 class 0-6-0 No. 2142 on loan to the GWR.

In March 1955, trials were conducted with unbanked trains of greater weight than the maximum of 90 tons to which an unassisted engine was permitted. For the trials, all trailing points and trap points on the incline were locked, so that if the train's weight drew the engine backwards, it would not become derailed.

Class 5 4-6-0 No. 44776, with a load of 222 tons, made the first run without incident. The second run demanded three stops and restarts. At the first, No. 44776 slipped violently but then got a grip and experienced no trouble with the further two restarts. Jubilee Class 6 4-6-0 No. 45554 *Ontario*, with a load of 252 tons successfully climbed with a non-stop run, but on the second run, after making four attempts at restarting, had to back down to Bromsgrove and start from there. It managed the second and third restarts on the incline. The third attempt on each Sunday was from a standing start at Bromsgrove, which both engines managed successfully. Jubilee class 4-6-0 No. 45699 *Galatea* once hauled fourteen bogie coaches up the incline. Although it started from Bromsgrove with two engines assisting in the rear, the first of these primed and so, necessarily, both had to stop. *Galatea* proceeded on her own and arrived punctually at New Street.

LNWR 0-8-4T No. 7953 was unsuccessfully tried in 1929/30 and LMSR 2-6-0 + 0-6-2 Garratt No. 4998 in 1934, when *Big Bertha* was in the shops at Derby. In 1949, Sir Nigel Gresley's 2-8-0 + 0-8-2 Garratt No. 69999, the most powerful steam locomotive in Great Britain, built specially for banking up the Worsborough Incline, was rendered redundant by electrification of that section. But as it was still a useful machine, BR looked around for new fields of operation and sent it to Bromsgrove and arrived on 7 March 1949. Initially, it banked chimney-first, but some guards complained of severe jolting when it buffered up. This was due to the difficulty of judging the distance because of its length and also drifting steam. On 10 March 1949, it was turned on the King's Norton–Lifford–Bournville triangle. Considered equal to three Class 3F 0-6-0Ts, unfortunately it was disliked by firemen due to its voracious appetite for coal and the false water gauge readings.

0-6-0WT No. 223, the Lickey banker for many years. Built at Derby in 1862, it was withdrawn as LMS No. 1607 in 1928. (*Collection of Revd W. Awdry*)

It required 10–12 cwts to be shovelled for each trip – very hard work for an inexperienced new young fireman – compared with the more moderate 6–7 cwt for *Big Bertha*, or only 5 cwt for a Class 3F 0-6-0T. Even after being equipped for oil burning in 1952, No. 69999 was still not successful, clouds of black, oily smoke drifting across a golf course and gardens. The ex-Caledonian Railway Pug No. 56020 was used to pump oil.

In January 1957, before the line was transferred to the Western Region, 9400 class 0-6-0PTs Nos 8400-6 took over banking duties. To bring them into line with what the footplate crew were used to, LMSR pattern continuous blow-down valves were fitted, together with LMSR lamp brackets. Sometimes as many as four of these bankers would be required on a goods train. Ex-GWR 2-8-0T No. 5226 arrived in 1958 and stayed for two years, while ex-GWR 2-8-2T No. 7235 was tried on 18 April 1958, but its cylinders fouled the platform at Bromsgrove.

On 20 September 1961, Type 4 diesel-electric No. D40 (later No. 45133) was tested up the incline with a load of sixteen coaches. Three tests were made: from a standing start south of Bromsgrove; from a standing start at Bromsgrove and from a flying start south of the station. Each climb took between six and eight minutes. The train was followed at a distance of 30–50 yards by BR Standard Class 9 2-10-0 No. 92234. The next day these tests were successfully repeated with goods wagons.

On 16 February 1961, tests were made with the experimental Brush diesel-electric D0280 *Falcon*. She made a successful climb with eighteen coaches and the Western Region dynamometer car, a total of 638 tons. Tests were then run with freight trains of 618 tons. In May and June 1961, prototype diesel-hydraulic D0260 *Lion* started 500 tons from dead stops on the incline. The result of these tests proved that banking was not compulsory in all cases.

By 1964, Class 37 diesel locomotives had taken over banking duties, the first being English Electric Type 3 (later termed Class 37) D6938 on 2 July 1964. In July 1966, tests were made with Hymek diesel-hydraulic locomotives, D7021 to D7025 ousting the Class 37s in November 1967. Since 13 September 1985, the two Class 37 bankers have only worked from 19.00 to 04.30, Mondays to Fridays, assisting freight trains and the Bristol to Glasgow sleeper. During the day, instead of standing under-used at Bromsgrove, one locomotive worked from Worcester during the day, with the other used on permanent way trains from either Gloucester or Worcester. The crews continued to book on at Bromsgrove, however, fetching and returning the locomotives to their stabling points. By 1987, Bromsgrove ceased to be a signing-on point and the bankers were based at Gloucester. In 2003, five Class 66 locomotives (Nos. 66055 to 66059) were equipped for Lickey banking duties, being given a downward-pointing light to assist buffering up at night and buckeye couplers released by air and swung to one side. These engines were based at Saltley and worked to and from Bromsgrove as required.

0-10-0 *Big Bertha* (21C, Bromsgrove) at Bromsgrove, September 1937. (*W. Potter*)

Regarding ordinary train engines working the line, from 1854, Kirtley 6-foot 8-inch 2-2-2 Nos. 120–9 worked expresses from Bristol to Birmingham but ceased in 1870 as a result of footplatemen sending a deputation to Kirtley, complaining that singles were incapable of working heavy trains over the steeply graded line. They were then replaced by 2-4-0 Nos. 820–9. These, in turn, were superseded in 1880 by Johnson 1282 class 2-4-0s. 1892 saw 4-2-2 singles working to Bristol, but these were replaced by 4-4-0s a few years later, although until the mid-1920s they could still be seen as train engines on reliefs as well as being utilised as pilots. During the First World War, South Eastern & Chatham Railway Nos. 58 and 359, together with Glasgow & South Western Railway No. 299a worked between Gloucester and Cheltenham.

4-4-0 Compounds and the 990 Class did not penetrate to Bristol before grouping, and the heaviest duties on the Devonian and the Newcastle and Bristol mails were performed by Class 3 4-4-0s, lighter expresses being hauled by a Class 2 4-4-0. Compounds were economical if a driver made use of compounding. John Stamp ran the 18 miles from Cheltenham to Abbot's Wood Junction without firing. Class 4 Compound 4-4-0s appeared in 1924 while Jubilee class 4-6-0s came ten years later, gradually taking over the heaviest trains. During the Second World War, Patriot class 4-6-0s, which had first appeared on the line in 1931, were given the heaviest train, the 7.40 a.m. from Bristol, always consisting of fifteen bogie coaches. Class 5 4-6-0s performed excellent work on Derby expresses hauling twelve coach trains; while Crab Class 5 2-6-0s were also used on passenger workings. Royal Scot No. 46120 *Royal Inniskilling Fusilier* appeared in February 1949.

Eastern Region B1 class 4-6-0s came on the scene in 1958, particularly on the Saturday 12.48 p.m. ex-York, returning the following day with the 4.45 p.m. to Bradford. A V2 class 2-6-2 sometimes appeared on this train, but technically this class was not cleared for working the route. Other ex-LNER engines recorded have been 2-6-0s of the K1 and K3 classes and 01 and 04 2-8-0s. J39 0-6-0 No. 64930 from Northwich shed appeared on 23 August 1959 and No. 64789 from Peterborough on 11 October 1959. These were not the first appearances of LNER engines on the line, as during the Second World War B12/3 class 4-6-0s, because of their wide route availability, were used on ambulance trains all over England. On 11 June 1944, soon after D-Day, No. 8555 and SR S11 class 4-4-0 No. 404 were seen between Gloucester and Cheltenham, while also on the same date, No. 8525 and 8549 were on separate trains, both piloted by LMS Class 2P 4-4-0s. On 14 June 1944, No. 8519 was seen piloted by a Class 4F 0-6-0.

With diesel power ousting steam on some other lines, Royal Scot and rebuilt Patriot 4-6-0s made their appearance, as did Stanier 2-6-0s. From the early 1960s, some trains rostered for diesel power occasionally reverted to steam power, particularly in the severe winter of 1962/63 when many diesel locomotives froze.

For many years, local passenger services were worked by 0-4-4Ts of the Kirtley or Johnson variety, but by 1933 most of the duties had been passed to Deeley 0-6-4Ts, nearly half of this class being shedded at Saltley.

Patriot Class 6 4-6-0 No. 45504 *Royal Signals* (82E, Bristol, Barrow Road) at Gloucester on 9 September 1960, comes off the Newcastle to Bristol express headed by Jubilee Class 6 4-6-0 No. 45685 *Barfleur*. (R.E. Toop)

In 1905, the MR gave each locomotive a power classification, the table showing the maximum number of goods wagons allowed for each type between Birmingham and Gloucester:

	Empty	Mineral	Goods
Class 1	50	38	50
Class 2	50	46	50
Class 3	50	50	50

Until the appearance of the Stanier 8F 2-8-0s, goods trains were worked by 0-6-0s, but in 1950 the Beyer Garratts from Toton, previously not used beyond King's Norton, began working to Westerleigh marshalling yard north of Bristol on an evening freight, returning next day on an early morning goods or empties. Occasionally an LNWR 0-8-0 put in an appearance. Steam lasted longer on freight than on passenger duties. The last steam working, apart from preserved engines, may well have been on 4 September 1966, when Class 9F 2-10-0 No. 92094 worked to Gloucester and then returned up the line light engine.

With the changeover to diesel working, Class 45 and 46 Peak engines appeared on expresses, together with Class 47, though over the years most BR diesel types have worked over the line. HSTs on some North East to South West services began on 1 October 1981 running to ordinary schedules, but from 17 May 1982 Bristol to Sheffield times were reduced by twenty minutes, Newcastle to Cardiff by nearly forty-five minutes and Plymouth to Edinburgh by two hours. Today, much of the excitement of the Lickey Incline is lost as HSTs often surmount the summit at speeds of over 60 mph.

Several contemporary accounts of locomotive working survive. On 10 July 1840, Moorsom wrote, 'The usual train on this railway comprises four passenger coaches and two trucks, being an ordinary gross weight of 45 tons, and with such trains as these, engines of Class B run on level grades at a speed of 34 mph, and sometimes they make as much as 38 mph without any difficulty arising out of the rapid action of the piston. On grades rising 1 in 300 they take the same train at a speed of 24 to 25 mph.'

R. G. Gaut, in *A History of Worcester Agriculture & Rural Evolution*, wrote that, 'Cattle trains on this line excited much curiosity in the autumn of 1840, these, on Thursdays and Saturdays, often consisted of fifty carriages laden with oxen, sheep and pigs drawn by three or four engines.'

Brush Type 4 diesel-electric D1658 speeds through Ashchurch with a Down freight, 15 September 1965. (*Revd Alan Newman*)

Locomotive Sheds

A small shed at Saltley, which became the Midland's principal Birmingham shed, was opened in 1839 by the Birmingham & Derby Junction Railway. The MR, requiring an adequate locomotive depot at Birmingham, in 1851 sought to extend it, though building did not commence until 1855; the twenty-four-road roundhouse was brought into use the following year. Within ten years, the shed proved too small, so another was opened on the opposite side of the tracks. The new shed opened in 1868, followed by another roundhouse in 1876, and the following year the very first shed was abandoned. Shed No. 3, another roundhouse, was built in 1900. Given Code 3 by the MR, in 1935 it became 21A under the LMS reorganisation and was provided with mechanical coaling and ash disposal plants. In the period following the Second World War, the three sheds were rebuilt, No. 1 and No. 2 sheds in concrete and No. 3 in steel and glass. Saltley was the London Midland Region's most important shed, with an allocation of 191 locomotives in 1954. In September 1963 it was recoded 2E. With the full electrification of the area, Saltley closed to steam on 6 March 1967, remaining open for diesels.

Bournville was a MR standard roundhouse built in brick and opened in 1895, the 50-foot turntable being replaced by one of 57 feet around 1948. In 1956, an engine fell into the pit, damaging the table, which was sent to Swindon for repair, locomotives temporarily using Saltley and Bromsgrove. Originally coded 3A, it became 21B in 1935 and was given 'garage' status. It closed on 14 February 1960.

The three-road stone-built shed at Bromsgrove was built alongside the works on the east side of the line at the foot of the incline, its principal purpose being to house and service banking engines. Until 1892, the turntable was on the shed's south road, but that year it was replaced by a 46-foot table at Bromsgrove South. Water for the shed tank was supplied from a bore hole, delivery being inside the shed, while a large reservoir cut into the red sandstone south of the Alveston Road bridge supplied both works and station. Until this reservoir was constructed, the railway had to pay an annual charge of £50 for water supply to the station.

The engines initially burned coke and this was made at Gloucester, but was wasteful as gas and other by-products were unused. In 1844, McConnell set up a gasworks at Bromsgrove, the gas illuminating both works and station, some being piped to Blackwell station and the remainder sold to the Bromsgrove Gas Company.

The shed closed on 27 September 1964, Bromsgrove works also closing with the loss of more than 200 jobs. The shed's original code was 4A, becoming 21C in 1934, 85F when transferred to the Western Region in February 1958 and 85D in January 1961. It closed on 27 September 1964.

The Midland had a road reserved at the Midland & South Western Junction Railway's Cheltenham shed. This three-road depot opened in December 1911 and closed December 1935.

The first brick-built shed at Gloucester was replaced on 8 July 1850 by a 150-foot-diameter roundhouse situated north of Barton Road level crossing

Class 3F 0-6-0 No. 43186 (21C, Bromsgrove) at its home shed, 16 April 1955. (*R. C. Riley*)

WD class 2-8-0 No. 90337 at Bromsgrove locomotive depot photographed from the footplate of Class 9 2-10-0 No. 92156. (*W. F. Grainger*)

Gloucester Barnwood shed, March 1964. The coaling stage is on the left. (*W. F. Grainger*)

between the transfer shed and passenger station, at a cost of £4,085 and an additional £965 for smithy and stores. The 35-foot-diameter table gave access to thirteen radial stalls, each 50 feet in length, six being standard gauge and seven mixed gauge. The table was enlarged in 1869, and by 1883 an additional 50-foot table had been provided in the yard.

When it was decided to replace the MR terminus by a through station (opened 12 April 1896), the site of the shed was required, so a new square building was erected at Barnwood, east of the Great Western shed at Horton Road. Equipped with a 50-foot turntable, it opened in 1895, a four-road fitting shop being added at a later date. North-west of the station a turntable, water crane and ash pit were installed at a cost of £1,301. The shed code 7 became 22B in 1935, the year a 55-foot table was installed. Its code in Western Region days was 85E, later 85C. The depot closed on 4 May 1964, locomotives and men being transferred to the nearby ex-GWR Horton Road shed.

Tewkesbury had a single-road brick-built shed, probably opened in the 1850s. It closed on 7 September 1962 but the building survived in industrial use until being demolished in February 1986. In 1863, a temporary corrugated-iron shed for one engine was erected at Ashchurch at a cost of £35, and in 1914 the coal stage received a new roof for £50. The shed closed by 1923.

Worcester shed, first opened in 1870, was rebuilt in timber in 1894 as a three-road brick building, code No. 4. It closed on 12 December 1932 and was

Gloucester Barnwood shed, 1963: Class 5 4-6-0 No. 45464, left, and ex-GWR 4-6-0 No. 6825 *Llanvair Grange*, right. (*W. F. Grainger*)

BR Standard Class 5 4-6-0 No. 73003 near the coaling stage, Barnwood, with a Class 4F 0-6-0 beyond. (*W. F. Grainger*)

Above: Class 2P 4-4-0 No. 40540 (22B, Gloucester) and Class 3F 0-6-0 No. 43599 at Barnwood, 9 August 1956. (*Revd Alan Newman*)

Left: Class 1F 0-6-0T No. 1876 (7, Gloucester) at its home shed, 4 March 1934. (*Revd Alan Newman*)

Swindon-built Class 8F 2-8-0 No. 48424 (21A, Saltley) at Barnwood, 26 June 1952. (*Revd Alan Newman*)

Class 3F 0-6-0 No. 43242 (21A, Saltley) and a Class 9 2-10-0 at Barnwood, 24 October 1961. (*Revd Alan Newman*)

demolished in the summer of 1939. When the shed shut, most of the Worcester turns were arranged to be worked by other depots, with the exception of one turn, which required a Gloucester Class 2P 4-4-0 to be sub-shedded at Worcester, arrangements made with the GWR to look after it at nights and weekends. When the Second World War emergency timetables came into force, further LMS locomotives began to make use of this facility.

2-4-0 No. 1295, with a train of London & North Western Railway coaches on 11 April 1896, forms the last train to leave the MR Gloucester terminus. (*Real Photographs*)

Chapter Four

Rolling Stock

BGR coaches, categorised into three classes, were hung low, only 2 feet 8 inches above rail level, the springs sited below the axle boxes and the wheels in 'paddle boxes' under the seats. First- and second-class coaches were ordered in 1839 from William Shackleford, Oxford, and F. & C. Arthur, Birmingham. First-class coaches had a coupé at each end, those used on the night mails having Imperials [trunks] on their roofs to accommodate the luggage. First-class coaches seated a total of eighteen passengers sitting three abreast. The average cost of a vehicle was £370.

Second-class coaches had three compartments, open above the dwarf partitions, the roof being supported by iron standards in the centre of each partition. They seated a total of twenty-four passengers sitting four abreast. The windows were unglazed until October 1844, and passengers were advised to wear goggles, frequently of fine mesh, hired or sold for the purpose The buffers and draw bar were on a special spring. A brake shoe for each wheel was worked by a system of levers, an upright rod terminating in a handle by the guard's seat in the open air at each end of the coach roof. First- and second-class coaches were painted in a livery of dark buff, picked out in black, the BGR coat of arms, comprising those of Birmingham and Gloucester, appearing on the centre doors. The average cost of a second-class coach was £190.

Third-class vehicles had neither seats nor roofs, but had an enclosed compartment for luggage in the centre, the standing berths being at each end. Surprisingly, it was said at the company's general meeting in August 1840, 'The passengers very generally have borne testimony to the comfort of the carriages and the peculiarly easy motion of the line.' Some had other opinions, one such being a contributor to *Herapath's Railway Journal*. He considered that the suspension was far from perfect, and that leg straps should be provided to prevent lighter passengers from taking aerial trips. By 1843, some third-class coaches were covered and offered seats, receiving praise from the *Railway Times* of October 1843 who said they were 'the only ones I have yet seen affording to the passengers that protection from wind and weather they have the right to expect. They are large covered wagons closed at the front and with the door behind. They have seats round and passengers can either stand up or sit down. The same company have also separated third class carriages with like accommodation for women and children.'

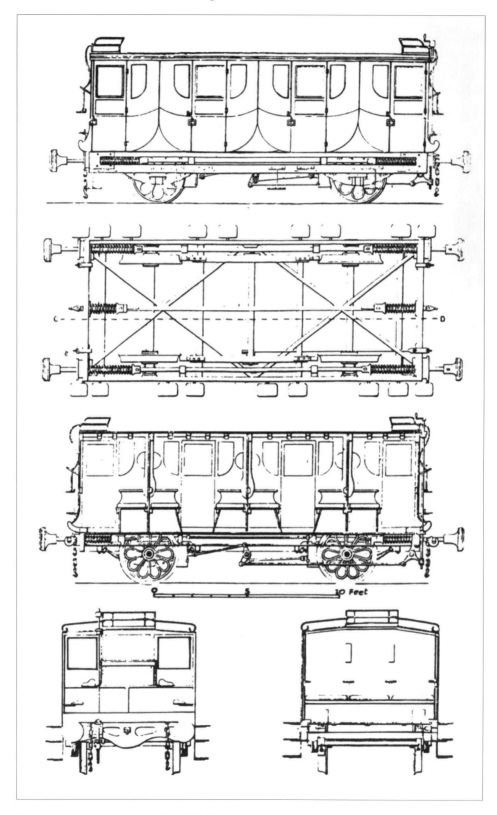

Drawing, plan and sections of a BGR first-class carriage of 1847.

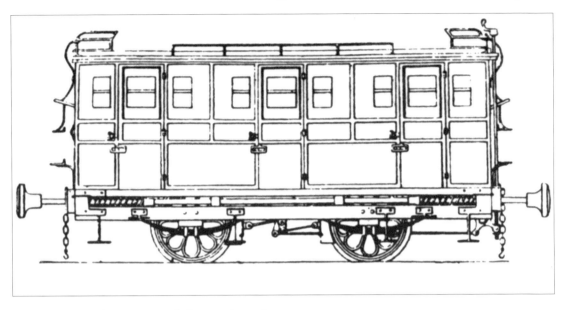

Drawing of a BGR second-class carriage of 1847.

In his report of 21 October 1840 to the Board of Trade, Captain Melluish said that the brake was the best he had seen. 'It is worked by a single or double winch fixed on a spindle at the top of the carriage and by turning the winch the brake is applied to all four wheels at the same time, and I should think the power nearly sufficient, if applied by a tolerably strong brakesman, to arrest almost entirely the rotation of the wheels. I am of the opinion it would tend greatly the safety of the public if the use of this description of brake were introduced on all lines of railway.'

King's Norton had carriage sidings where some of the rush hour stock was kept and trains carrying visitors to Cadbury's in Bournville were maintained here. Older stock used for excursions was also stabled at King's Norton. Trains from New Street to various destinations originated from King's Norton and during the Second World War, when the few holiday trains were overcrowded, those in the know and wishing to travel to, say, Llandudno joined the train at King's Norton rather than New Street.

In 1896, the MR ordered three sets of six coaches at a cost of £16,800 for Bradford to Bristol traffic. Each train consisted of a six-wheeled guard's van; twelve-wheeled third-class carriage; twelve-wheeled third-class dining car; six-wheeled kitchen car with luggage space; twelve-wheeled composite first-class dining carriage and finally a twelve-wheeled brake composite. They began work on 2 August 1897 on the 1.25 p.m. Bradford to Bristol and the 2.05 p.m. Bristol to Bradford, the third set being a spare. There were no less than five classes of passenger on these trains – first and third diners; first and third non-diners with lavatories, and third non-diners without lavatories. The total time of the stops made was fifty-two minutes, and it kept a steady average speed of 45–48 mph station to station. Between Derby and Bristol it was hauled by a 7-foot 6-inch single.

On 14 January 1841, for the first time, a Travelling Post Office carriage and tender, together with a parcels sorting carriage, ran at 7.00 p.m. from Bristol to Camp Hill, while the corresponding Down train ran to Bristol. The 1903 Post Office list shows carriage used by Bristol sorters between Derby and Bristol called the Bristol Sorting Carriage, but this is not mentioned in the 1899 and 1908 lists, sorters presumably then working in the Midland TPO.

BGR goods stock originally had dumb buffers. During 1844 and 1845, nearly 300 new wagons were ordered. They had five-plank sides and ends, a single brake lever and cost an average of £60 each. The BGR wagon works was at Bromsgrove, and under the MR it became the main wagon repair centre for that company.

MR third class coach used for Birmingham to Gloucester services, *c.* 1874. Notice the side chains provided for security in addition to the central coupling. A luggage rack is provided outside on the roof. (*Author's collection*)

Chapter Five

Working the Lickey Incline

At the Lickey Incline, the railway climbs the scarp, a tunnel being out of the question because the gentle dip slope beyond the summit would have required its length to have been excessive. The incline's claim to fame lies not in that it is steeper or longer than any other gradient, but that it lies on a main line. For instance in 1904, sixty trains in each direction used the plane every twenty-four hours, excluding specials or descending bank engines. Trains were not short, again quoting 1904, expresses frequently consisting of a dozen heavy bogie vehicles. T. R. Perkins, writing in the *Railway Magazine* that year, says of Blackwell station at the head of the incline where all trains stopped for brakes to be tested,

Class 3F 0-6-0T No. 47308, left, and No. 47303, right, banking a passenger train near the summit of the Lickey Incline, 20 August 1949. No. 47303 is lettered 'British Railways'. Brackets on the bunkers were for carrying route boards when working passenger trains in the London area. (*W. Potter*)

0-10-0 No. 58100 and four Class 3F 0-6-0Ts on 20 August 1949, running light down the Lickey Incline just below Blackwell. (*W. Potter*)

0-10-0 No. 58100 banking a passenger train near Blackwell, 20 August 1949. The last coaches are ex-GWR stock. (*W. Potter*)

The view from the platforms at this station is a striking one; the railway appears to drop into space over the edge of the bank, and it is necessary to go to the extreme end of the station to trace its onward course. Far below, where the shining lines of steel appear to converge to a point, a puff of steam from the shunting yard marks the position of Bromsgrove station at the foot of the incline, while the Malvern hills stand out boldly on the horizon immediately above the railway. A few yards from the platform stands a gradient-post, showing the change of gradient from 1 in 305 to 1 in 37½. For 2 miles and a furlong the 'bank' extends, the line being perfectly straight for the entire distance. Blackwell station stood 556 ft above sea level while Bromsgrove station is only at 300 ft.

During the BGR period, all Up trains were required to stop at Bromsgrove so that the bank engine could be coupled in front – not assisted in the rear – while carriages and wagons were properly connected by both centre and side chains. When the last vehicle was over the summit, while still on the move, the fireman climbed and uncoupled the bank engine, the trip hook being detached by his foot. This modification, invented by J. E. McConnell, obviated the need for the fireman to climb over the tender to release the coupling. The driver of the train engine then shut off the steam so that the bank engine could accelerate at least 30 yards ahead and be turned into a special siding, the points then being hastily set for the main line. After the train passed, the bank engine descended to Bromsgrove at a speed not exceeding 12 mph. From 1 May 1842, the saddle tank bank engines

Two Class 3F 0-6-0Ts bank a passenger train, September 1941. (*Author's collection*)

An Up train of empty mineral wagons approaching Blackwell, *c.* 1924, behind Class 2P 4-4-0 No. 457. (*Author's collection*)

alone worked trains on the incline. They still uncoupled on the move and ran into a siding, while an engine waited on the main line to take the train forward. When Blackwell became a locomotive depot, coke was brought up from Bromsgrove in wagons coupled to any convenient train and then returned by gravity.

Perkins describes an Up passenger train around 1900, the speed of which reached a very respectable 30 mph soon after leaving Bromsgrove and was maintained to the summit:

> In front is, perhaps, a stately 'single', gliding along with little apparent effort; immediately behind it may be another of the same class, or maybe a four-coupled passenger engine, which appears to be doing a little more work than its neighbour; then come the long crimson carriages, and, last of all, bellowing away as if *they* at any rate cannot afford to lose any time, the two 'bankers', full of rage and fury, and vomiting clouds of steam and smoke. At the summit of the incline the bellowing suddenly stops, the 'bankers' drop off, and the express, gathering speed each moment, proceeds on its way; in a few moments the signal drops, the two tank engines cross to the Down line and make their way without steam back to Bromsgrove, and quiet reigns, though not for long, upon the Lickey incline.

Banking was compulsory for all passenger trains of 90 tons or over, and all freight trains of eight or more loaded mineral wagons or the equivalent, because in the

Class 9 2-10-0 No. 92156 begins the ascent of the Lickey Incline, 6 November 1963. (*W. F. Grainger*)

A little further up. (*W. F. Grainger*)

event of a coupling snapping, a brake van may have been unable to hold runaways on the formidable gradient. Information regarding the number of bankers required for a train was given by the driver to the signalman at Stoke Works Junction, who passed it on to Bromsgrove South signal box.

The following code was used:

		Driver's whistle code to Stoke Works Jc. signalman	Stoke Works Jc. signalman's code to Bromsgrove south box when train enters section
Freight train requiring:	1 banker	1-1 short	2-3-2
	2 bankers	1-2 short	2-2-2
	more than 2 bankers	1-3 short	Advised by telegraph

When a train halted at Bromsgrove, the banker carefully approached. In fog or falling snow, the engine had to be guided to the rear of the train by a 'competent person' in order that it was not struck violently. The signalman at Bromsgrove station box was instructed not to clear his signals until he received the 'assisting engine in rear of train' bell from the South box, which had a better sighting of the operation, to indicate that the banker had buffered up, uncoupled, to the rear of the train. The clearing of the signals by Bromsgrove station box indicated to the driver of the train engine that the banker was in position, and he would then whistle to indicate a start. The signalman at the station box illuminated the 'Right Away' indicator and seeing this, the bank engine driver opened his regulator.

From 2 February 1914, trains requiring assistance and not booked to call at Bromsgrove station received banking from the South box, whereas previously all trains had been assisted in the rear from the station causing difficulty in starting at the foot of the incline.

The two-road bank section was fed from both ends by quadruple tracks. On 27 April 1930, a new signal box at Blackwell was brought into use; a bank engine siding put in between the Up and Down roads and a Lickey Signal installed. This was a special signal, neither fully automatic, nor an ordinary intermediate block signal. It was a two-aspect colour light with repeating distant and operated so that in the ordinary course of events, no train would be stopped on the bank.

The Lickey Signal automatically went red when the train entered a track section 300 yards in advance. With a long train, this meant that the signal could go to danger in front of the bank engine. After a train had cleared Blackwell inner home, the lever which worked the Lickey Bank signal could be put to 'off', but the signal would not actually clear to green until the previous train had cleared the inner home signal beyond Blackwell platform. The introduction of this automatic signal increased the traffic capacity of the incline by 40 per cent and reduced delays by 57 per cent.

During the Second World War, this automatic signal was the means of revealing theft. At one time, tobacco was stolen from sealed Wills' tobacco vans.

Passing Bromsgrove's Down distant signals.

Meeting sister engine No. 92000 with a Down freight.

Illumination from the intermediate colour light signal revealed thieves throwing it out as the train slowly ascended the Lickey Incline, the tobacco being thrown out to a lane running beside the railway on its west side.

Acceptance of a train depended on the type of train being offered by the Bromsgrove signalman to Blackwell and the type of train already in the section. For example, any train could be accepted when an express reached the Lickey Signal; an express following a train stopping at Blackwell could not be accepted until it has passed the inner home. To facilitate this method of working, a train describer was in use between Bromsgrove and Blackwell on the Up road to indicate a fast, slow passenger train, or freight. In the event of the describer's failure, the signalman could institute normal block working, making the Lickey Signal inoperative, although the aspect still showed. Blackwell had calling-on arms under both outer and inner Up home signals so that a train could creep off the worst of the gradient. It was an operational advantage that the heaviest loads tended to be down rather than up the incline.

In *The Lickey Incline*, H. C. Casserley tells of a day in April 1958 when Compound 4-4-0 No. 41090 arrived at Bromsgrove with three non-corridor coaches. Ex-GWR 0-6-0PT No. 8404 was provided for banking assistance, but the Compound's driver, determined to show what his machine could do, set off at full blast using high pressure steam in all three cylinders. So fast was his acceleration that the banker was unable to keep up with him. Casserley wrote, 'The spectacle of the pannier tank trying to catch up with the train it was supposed to be assisting was laughable in the extreme.' He estimated that No. 41090 maintained a speed of 35 mph all the way up the bank.

Partly permissive working was allowed on the Down road when a freight, and only a freight, was descending the incline. Just bankers were allowed to follow when a subsidiary arm fixed below the Blackwell advanced starter was pulled off showing 'C' or 'W'. 'C' (calling-on) appeared in the display when the track circuit cleared immediately in front of the starting signal, and when a freight train was approximately three-quarters of the way down the bank, a 'W' [warning] could appear in the display.

Bromsgrove station, 1½ miles from the parish church, had two platform roads with a centre road for non-stop Down trains. Until the 1890s, all Down trains were required to halt at the station, but then a limit of 10 mph was imposed through the station. Passenger trains from Blackwell to Bromsgrove were required to take at least five minutes and goods trains twelve minutes for the distance of just over 2 miles.

Brake levers of all wagons were required to be dropped at Blackwell and then one in every two or three, depending on the weight of their contents, pinned down. Brakesmen took their places and pinned down the brakes as the train slowly passed them. A brakesman was on duty at Blackwell continuously, except between 6.00 a.m. and 10.00 p.m. on Sundays. When he was not on duty, guards were required to see that the regulations were kept. As a result of the friction of the brakes on the wheels and the wheels on the rails, the ballast of the down line throughout the length of the incline was covered with minute particles of iron,

No. 92156 nears the summit and enters mist.

giving it a reddish-brown appearance, very different from the Up line.

To indicate the summit, the BGR fixed a post bearing a white light, lit at night and in fog. Here, in the days before continuous brakes, passenger trains were required to stop and whistle for the brakesmen in addition to sounding the usual three sharp whistles for guards to apply the brakes. On the incline, the brakesmen took charge, the first brakesman being on the middle coach, the second brakesman, guards and porters taking positions ordered by the first brakesman, the fireman positioning himself by the tender brake. Speed of descending passenger trains was limited to 20 mph, or 16 mph in slippery weather, goods trains being restricted to 10 mph.

Brakesmen used the following hand whistle code:

No. of Whistles
1. Start train.
2. Shut off steam when train has started.
3. Apply brakes. If repeated on the gradient means 'Apply brakes more forcibly'.
4. Ease brakes gradually.
5. Obstruction at foot of gradient.

GWR 94XX class 0-6-0PT No. 8400 and No. 8405 at Bromsgrove, 15 August 1964. The notice on the left reads, 'Passengers must not cross the line except by means of the footbridge'. (*Richard Brown*)

Class 9 2-10-0 No. 92139 (21A, Saltley) passes Blackwell with an Up freight. (*Author's collection*)

INSTRUCTIONS RELATING TO TABLES OF MAXIMUM LOADS

Accelerated Timings.—The letters A T in the Loading Tables indicate the loading applicable to trains marked A T in the columns of the Passenger Working Time Table.

Assisting Engines.—In the event of the authorised loading of passenger trains being exceeded, assisting engines will be arranged as necessary from Divisional Headquarters, and information will be given to drivers when assistance is being provided.

The following are the instructions for banking passenger trains from Bromsgrove to Blackwell and Bristol to Fishponds.

BROMSGROVE TO BLACKWELL

	Load in tons Class of Engine				
	2	3	4	5	6
Unassisted	90	90	90	90	90
Assisted by one Class 3 Freight Tank bank engine ...	195	215	230	250	270
Assisted by two Class 3 Freight Tank bank engine or one 0-10-0 Class bank engine...	295	315	330	350	370

When these loads are exceeded, three class 3 Freight Tank bank engines or one 0-10-0 class bank engine and one class 3 Freight Tank bank engine are necessary, except that double-headed trains may take up to 250 tons with one class 3 Freight Tank bank engine.

Maximum loads of passenger trains, issued on 1 November 1954.

F. S. Williams wrote in 1876:

> In years gone by, a heavy mineral train has been known, with all its brakes on, and its wheels spragged, to sweep unhindered down the incline through Bromsgrove station, and to run a mile and more away along the flat line at the foot before its course could be arrested. At night, too, the sight has sometimes been strange. The wheels being spragged, and not turning, of course the particular part that pressed on the rail became hotter and hotter, so hot as to throw off fibres and flakes of molten metal twisted into all conceivable forms and every wheel sent out a blaze of heat and light so as almost to make the train appear to be on fire. 'I have seen,' said a gentleman to the writer, 'tons of bits of metal, that have thus been burned off the old iron tires (sic), lying on the ballast of the Lickey Incline.'

With the adoption of continuous brakes, descending the incline still needed care, but the compulsory brake testing stop at Blackwell was abolished on 10 November 1943, though passenger and fully fitted freight trains were restricted to a speed of 10 mph through Blackwell station and were required to descend the incline in not less than five minutes. Light engines were required to halt at the summit before proceeding. Bank engines were not coupled together when descending the incline, but brought together at the head of the descent and the handbrake of the leading engine applied. The rear engine, or engines, then propelled the leading locomotive

No. 45064 climbs the Lickey Incline, 4 June 1983, with an Up express consisting of Eastern Region coaches. (*Author*)

on to the incline and the brakes of all the engines were used to prevent them from being separated until arrival at Bromsgrove.

Train drivers requiring to use the water column at Bromsgrove South stopped short and then carefully drew forward, because it they overshot, it was almost impossible to reverse up the gradient.

It is believed that the first instance of ex-GWR engines working up the Lickey Incline was on 16 September 1950 when No. 2937 *Clevedon Court* and No. 2920 *Saint David* drew an excursion from Hereford through to Bournville. The eleven bogie coaches and two vans were banked up the Lickey by *Big Bertha*.

The introduction of diesel traction reduced the need for banking assistance. The first DMU set to ascend the incline was on 2 June 1957 when an eight-car set returning from an excursion to Weston-super-Mare ascended in four minutes, with a minimum of 26 mph reached at Blackwell. The last regular steam banking engines ceased operation in June 1965, though on 7 October 1965 when Type 3 English Electric D6939 was derailed; for the rest of the day it was replaced by 4-6-0 No. 6947 *Helmingham Hall*.

In diesel days, Bromsgrove was signalled from Gloucester power box. When a train needed banking, it was brought to a stop either on the main line or the loop just south of Bromsgrove station. The driver pressed a plunger, which informed the Gloucester box that he was ready to depart. Meanwhile, when the train to be banked passed the bankers' siding, the bankers were signalled under permissive block to follow the train. When the banker was in position, a member of the banker's crew pressed one of the lineside plungers. This started a time release of fifteen seconds and at the end of this period the signal cleared. A gantry light illuminated RA (Right Away) for the relevant road. If the train was booked to call at Bromsgrove, or failed on the incline, a crow signal was used to start.

The last regular passenger train to be banked was the 21.25 Bristol to Glasgow and Edinburgh sleeper, but in the summer of 1988 it was divided into two parts, one starting from Plymouth and the other from Poole, the two uniting at New Street and no longer requiring assistance.

In July 2001, Voyager No. 220004 topped the incline at over 70 mph. The driver of a Down passenger train tests his brakes before Bromsgrove because, if a locomotive hauled train, it could be possible that the brake pipes had not been connected while with an HST sometimes the disc brakes froze.

The earliest runaway seems to have taken place in February 1841 when workmen at the Bromsgrove locomotive factory saw a wagon laden with quarry stone speeding down the incline at an estimated speed of almost 100 mph. They were unable to stop it, but another group of workmen 3 miles to the south saw it approaching. They had the presence of mind to secure scotches and lay them on the rail a short disatance apart and they were scarcely put down before the wagon reached the first. They halted it without derailment. The runaway had been caused by being nudged over the top of the incline by a carriage or engine.

Later that same year, several wagons began to roll unattended down the incline. A nine-year-old boy saw them and had the perspicacity to jump aboard and apply the brake. Realising he needed help he yelled for assistance. His mother heard, jumped on the train and, between them, they brought it safely to a halt.

Chapter Six

The Gloucester & Cheltenham Tramway

Although its route was not utilised by the BGR between Gloucester and Cheltenham, the tramroad should be mentioned. The development of Cheltenham as a spa some 200 years ago caused a rise in the demand for building stone and coal. On 28 April 1809, Parliament granted powers, 49 George III cap 23, for making a tramroad from Gloucester Quay to Knapp Toll Gate, Cheltenham, now Market Road, with a branch to the top of Leckhampton Hill. The first stone sleeper block was ceremonially laid by the Earl of Suffolk & Berkshire on 21 November 1809, and the branch from Leckhampton to Cheltenham opened on 2 July 1810, the line to Gloucester being inaugurated on 4 June 1811 and causing the price of coal at Cheltenham to fall from £1 15s 0d a ton to £1 4s 0d.

As insufficient capital was available to pay for the cost of constructing the line, an Act of 55 George III cap 41 of 12 May 1815 allowed the raising of £15,000 to clear a debt. Traffic developed, with 6,279 wagons running to Gloucester between 26 January 1824 and 19 June 1825, each wagon carrying a load of about two tons. By the mid-1830s, coal traffic over the whole line averaged 25,000 tons annually and the company paid dividends of 6–7 per cent.

The BGR cast covetous eyes on the tramroad as it offered access to Gloucester Docks. Samuel Bowly of the BGR met tramway representatives Lord Sherborne and George Newmarch early in January 1836. Another meeting was held on 18 January when Lord Suffolk deputised for Lord Sherborne, and as a result of this talk Bowly 'conceived his Lordship would be disposed to recommend the acceptance of £30,000 in cash'. In the event, the Cheltenham & Great Western Union Railway came forward with an offer of £35,000, which was accepted. The following day, the BGR and CGWUR agreed to construct a joint line between Cheltenham and Gloucester and share the cost of the tramroad purchase and early in 1837 the tramway was managed by three representatives from each railway company.

Between 1834 and 1842, tramroad traffic was intensive, averaging sixty journeys daily in each direction, with 35,000 tons of coal, roadstone and sundries annually – in addition to the 23,000 tons of stone carried over the Leckhampton branch.

The BGR's Cheltenham Lansdown station was sited near the tramway junction, and as the BGR was required to construct the half-mile-long Queen's Road to this station, the BGR was compelled to purchase the tramroad toll house and weighing machine, which stood in the road's path. As Lansdown was over a mile from the town centre, a proposal was made to lay a standard gauge line from the station alongside the tramroad to the tramway's Cheltenham depot, but the idea proved abortive.

In 1840, as the CGWUR was in severe financial difficulties and unable to fund its share of the Cheltenham to Gloucester main line, the BGR otained an Act in 1838 enabling it to purchase the CGWUR's share of the work done, complete the line and in addition purchase the CGWUR's share of the tramroad. The tramroad's managing committee was then reduced to five members, all BGR directors.

The opening of the BGR to Gloucester in November 1840 did not greatly affect the tramway as the BGR station at Cheltenham was rather remote from the town. Forest of Dean coal was highly popular, but the BGR had no access to this commodity. On 23 August 1841, the BGR built a 250-yard spur from the tramway to its Gloucester station in order that goods could be carried from the docks to to the railway more easily. This was not a very satisfactory solution as it still required transhipment between tramway and railway. In September 1842, the BGR planned to straddle the tramroad's High Orchard branch with standard gauge rails, but the bill failed to pass Parliament.

As traffic developed and the tramroad became inadequate, this scheme was revived in 1843. However, that year the GWR took over the CGWUR, and Brunel insisted that both broad and standard gauge rails should straddle the tramroad. The complexity of the three-gauge points would have been interesting.

Towards the end of May 1844, standard gauge rails reached the docks, but the tramroad was still very much in business; in the year ending April 1845, the tramway conveyed no less than 45,000 tons of goods. It could not be used for all traffic from the docks, and 5,000 long baulks of timber had to be carried through the streets of Gloucester as they were too lengthy to negotiate the tramway's tight curves. In 1845, the GWR exercised its right to repurchase a half share in the tramroad.

The BGR sought powers for building a better standard gauge line to the docks and a branch to High Orchard, the Act being granted in June 1845 after the company had been taken over by the Midland Railway. Its new owners were in no haste to use these powers, rails to High Orchard and the docks not being fully opened until 1848, but from this date traffic on the tramway saw a contraction. Certainly part of the standard gauge line, namely that from Barton Street level crossing to Rignum Place, was opened for locomotive working in mid-September 1847, as it was the scene of a tragic accident.

Horses drew wagons from the docks to Rignum Place, where a locomotive completed haulage to Gloucester goods station. The locomotive used was not fitted with an ash box and dropped live cinders on the line, which for years had been used as a public footpath. Ann Williams, aged six, played with some of these hot embers and while doing so, another cinder behind her set fire to her frock causing fatal injuries.

Thomas Knowles, the Gloucester Locomotive Superintendent, gave details at the inquest of the line's working. The engine used the branch between four and twelve times daily, one man riding on the front buffer beam and another travelling behind on a low truck attached to the engine, it being their duty to keep children from following or getting in the way of the engine. If the locomotive failed to clear all the wagons from the road at Rignum Place by the time the dock gates closed at 7 p.m., the engine made a further trip, but using lights, one lamp being fixed to the engine, the two men each carrying a hand lamp. The man in front dismounted before Barton Street crossing and signalled if the line was clear. The engine could be stopped in an average distance of 12 yards and sometimes in 4 or 5 yards.

From 1845, traffic on the tramroad gradually decreased as the MR brought coal from the Midlands, while the opening of the South Wales Railway in July 1854 offered coal direct from the Forest of Dean, though right until the tramway closed, some coal was still carried to Cheltenham by tram wagons returning from Gloucester Docks having delivered stone from Leckhampton Quarry. After 1854, the company's income only just exceeded expenditure. Its tracks caused a hazard to other road users and closure was pressed for, the Gloucester & Cheltenham Tramroads Abandonment Act being obtained on 1 August 1859. The Act having been granted, the authorities seemed in no haste to implement it. The line was eventually auctioned on 19 April 1861, most of the L-shaped tramway plate rails going to Forest of Dean buyers; the Cheltenham depot was sold on 9 July and that at Gloucester ten days later.

The permanent way was laid to 3-foot 6-inch gauge, the 3-foot-long cast-iron plates weighing about 46 lb, held to stone sleeper blocks by iron spikes driven into wooden plugs. At level crossings, flanges of plates were not supposed to protrude more than an inch above the road surface. Most of the sleeper blocks were of hard sandstone from the Forest of Dean. Although drivers were required by byelaw to walk beside their horses, the temptation to ride was irresistible. Shafts were fixed to the front of the tram by a transom pin and the breakage of a pin threw a driver sitting on the shafts in front of the wagon, the consequence likely to prove serious. This happened in September 1848, the *Cheltenham Examiner* reporting, 'Deceased was in the employ of Mr Jordan, coal merchant ... He had been repeatedly warned by his master not to ride on the shafts on pain of dismissal from his service; but in spite of these warnings he persisted in this common but dangerous practice'.

It was not only drivers who received injuries. In October 1827, 'a little boy named Samuel Poulton was riding on a railway tram loaded with coal, one of the large pieces was shook off, which fell upon his thigh and fractured it.' 'Thomas Fletcher, a little boy about seven years of age, was left to take care of five trams on the railway road, when endeavouring to stop the horses, he by some means got underneath and they went over him.'

Two loaded trams were the maximum load for one horse, a return trip of 17 miles from Cheltenham to Gloucester and back being a day's work. Loaded trams had precedence over empties as starting a loaded train from rest required much energy. Thus empty trains were required to wait in a passing loop for an oncoming loaded train.

Benjamin Newmarch, who had leased the tolls on the line, made an abortive trial of a novel steam locomotive. The patent of an American Major McCurdy, instead of having a conventional boiler, which in those days of primitive technology was liable to explode, steam was generated on the flash principle whereby a small volume of water in a coil was turned instantly to steam – rather on the principle of some gas-fired water heaters. The design failed through its inability to produce sufficient steam. During the winter of 1831/32, *Royal William* was tried, a conventional 0-6-0 designed by Henry Taylor and built by Neath Abbey Ironworks in 1831. The engine had no brakes, and to stop, it was placed in reverse. To hold a train on an incline, the wheels were spragged. The locomotive was enclosed to within a foot of the ground in a wooden box to prevent the machinery frightening horses.

In 1896 an elderly resident recalled in the *Gloucestershire Echo* of 24 December 1896 that the *Royal William* frequently derailed, was manhandled back on the track and never actually reached Cheltenham. Although the locomotive was a success, the permanent way was of insufficient strength to support it and the experiment was abandoned, horses continuing to be used. C. E. Stretton, not an historian famed for accuracy, in *Engineering* (1897, page 352) claims that in 1839/40 J. E. McConnell put flanged tyres on the wheels and eventually *Royal William* was broken up at Bromsgrove around 1842.

Medallion struck to commemorate the *Royal William* locomotive running on the Gloucester & Cheltenham Railway. (*Author's collection*)

Chapter Seven

The Cheltenham to Gloucester Main Line

The Cheltenham & Great Western Union Railway obtained its Act (6 & 7 William IV cap 77) on 21 June 1836. It was empowered, among other things, to build a line from Gloucester to Cheltenham, the BGR paying half the costs and controlling the northern half of the section. The BGR was to build a station at Gloucester for joint use, the CGWUR erecting one at Cheltenham. The gauge was to be that of the BGR, and as the CGWUR had adopted the broad gauge, it was required to lay broad gauge rails at its own expense, but after having laid them, each was to keep all rails in its half in good repair. After the passing of the Act, money was in short supply, so little progress could be made by the CGWUR. In an Extension of Time Act (1838), it was stated that if the Gloucester to Cheltenham line was not completed by 24 June 1840, the BGR would build the line itself, the Act also providing that each company should make its own station at Gloucester. The following year, the companies decided to have separate stations at Cheltenham.

The BGR planned to reach Gloucester Docks by an expensive viaduct and terminate at or near Commercial Road. Money being short, plans were revised and as the CGWUR also wanted an economical station at Gloucester and as works on the BGR were more forward than the CGWUR, the former agreed to buy a site and sell 3 acres on the north side at cost price when required.

Late in 1839, the CGWUR suggested that the BGR take over the Gloucester to Cheltenham line. The following year, the BGR concurred and arranged with the CGWUR to pay off the money that had been spent on it, this being carried out in monthly instalments of £20,000. This meant that the BGR was required to raise more money, as the whole, and not only half, the cost of the Gloucester to Cheltenham line had to be paid. Completion of the line to Gloucester was something of an embarrassment, as it involved the use of funds intended for the completion of stations and the purchase of locomotives and carriages. The line was handed over to the BGR on 18 June 1840, only six days before opening the railway from Bromsgrove to Cheltenham. On 17 October 1840, two experimental trips were made between Cheltenham and Gloucester and hundreds arrived to see the sight. A free ride was given from Gloucester to Cheltenham and back, the *Gloucester Journal* describing the carriages as 'handsome and commodious'.

Captain Melhuish of the Royal Engineers made the Board of Trade inspection on 21 October 1840. He found the earthworks safe and sound, but the permanent way incomplete. He observed that station clocks were placed conspicuously and could be seen from a train; watches were provided for enginemen and a timetable was placed on the engine, enabling a driver to check on timekeeping. The Cheltenham to Gloucester line was finally inaugurated on 4 November 1840 as part of the BGR. The *Railway Times* reported, 'We had the pleasure of travelling by railway to Gloucester starting at Lansdown at 9.00 we arrived in sixteen minutes. There was a large concourse of people awaiting the arrival who appeared much gratified with the new system of travelling. The prospects on the journey are delightful, having in view the Leckhampton and Churchdown Hills nearly the whole of the distance.'

The fact that the station at Cheltenham was a mile from the centre of the town was a disadvantage. The *Gloucester Journal* of 7 November 1840 reported,

> An abuse exists. At Lansdown Station the trains discharge Cheltenham passengers. Here each passenger can either walk or take a carriage to town; charge 6d, but if he has the slightest item of luggage the charge is 1s. This will certainly raise the prejudice in favour of the old method of transport – who will pay 2s first class fare plus 1s, [Gloucester to Cheltenham] when he gets horse vehicles door to door for 2s?

On 1 July 1843, the Great Western Railway took over the CGWUR still under construction between Swindon and Gloucester. This amalgamation was sanctioned by the Great Western Act of 1844, which authorised a 1¼-mile-long extension from the end of the joint line at Cheltenham Lansdown to a GWR station at St James' Square.

In 1844, the GWR paid the BGR half the cost of the Cheltenham to Gloucester line and laid broad gauge rails, the inner rails being common, instead of the outer as was later practice, in order to bring coaches of both gauges to the platform, but as there was no intermediate station between Gloucester and Cheltenham at this period, it was of no account. As it was the first important instance in England of a mixed gauge railway, on 11 October 1847 it was carefully inspected by Captain J. L. Simmons on behalf of the Railway Commissioners. The first broad gauge train service began on 23 October 1847. A short single line from Gloucester station met the new line at right angles, forming a T-junction. This was known as Gloucester T station, and connection between the two lines was made by turntable, this quaint method of working Gloucester traffic continuing until September 1851. The Cheltenham to Gloucester line was divided by a board west of Churchdown station, the Cheltenham half, including Churchdown station, being owned by the GWR, and the Gloucester part by the MR. Each company maintained its own section 'for the free and equal use of the other company without charge'.

In 1941/42, to cope with additional wartime traffic, the Gloucester to Cheltenham section was quadrupled at a cost of £50,000, works being carried out by Sir Robert McAlpine Ltd under supervision of the LMS from Gloucester to the halfway post just west of Churchdown and by the GWR for the remainder of the distance. Each railway used its own standards, so that the GWR length had lower quadrant signals, and the LMS upper quadrant semaphores with colour light distants. There were two series of mileposts on the line: those of the LMSR on the east side showing the mileage from Derby and those of the GWR on the west side from zero at Engine Shed Junction, Gloucester. The LMS regarded Cheltenham to Gloucester as Down, while the GWR considered it Up. As from 23 August 1942 the GWR gave way and it was generally agreed to be considered Down from Cheltenham to Gloucester. At least as recently as 1940, one of the stones on the Up side of an overbridge just north of Churchdown station was clearly engraved: 'C. & G. W. Union Railway – this Bridge was built Feby and March 1839'. With the reduction in traffic due to the development of road transport, the two relief roads were taken out in 1966/67.

In 1991, when an Up train was due to call at Cheltenham, the signal was always red in order that traffic could still cross the manned level crossing to the north. When the station work was completed, a plunger was pressed on the platform, which warned the signalman at Alstone Crossing to close the gates. In 1990, his box was struck by an HST when it went through the blocks in fog, requiring the timber of the lower half of the box to be replaced.

The Worcester Branch

An Act of 5 May 1837, 7 William IV cap 26, authorised branches from Wadborough to Worcester, and Ashchurch to Tewkesbury, but powers lapsed before active steps were taken, Worcester being served by a horse-drawn omnibus running to and from the BGR at Spetchley. Worcester felt badly let down because when the BGR went to Parliament it was agreed that the city was to have a station. The BGR was to have entered into a bond of £70,000 to enable the citizens to build a branch if the company failed to do so, yet the BGR had neither given the bond or built the branch.

When the BGR opened its first length, Worcester was marooned 3 miles from the railway at Spetchley. The citizens of Worcester were to a certain extent appeased by a free bus service, which met all trains. At a general meeting of the BGR in February 1842, complaints were made regarding the great expense of running these buses and the unsatisfactory way in which the public was conveyed, this giving rise to the consideration of constructing a branch line.

A bill in 1843 to raise capital of £25,000 for building such a line failed to pass Standing Orders. A special general meeting on 31 October 1844 authorised the application to Parliament for powers for a deviation line from Abbot's Wood through Worcester and Droitwich to Stoke, and a line from Droitwich to Wolverhampton with capital of £500,000. In the event, the Oxford, Worcester & Wolverhampton Railway (OWWR) received an Act (8 & 9 Victoria cap 184) of 4 August 1845 to build a line from Oxford through Evesham and Worcester to Wolverhampton, stipulating the provision of mixed gauge. On 5 October 1850, a single line between Abbot's Wood Junction on the main BGR line and a temporary station at Worcester, Shrub Hill, was opened and worked by the MR, although the property of the OWWR.

Initially, trains ran from Worcester to Spetchley, the exchange station at Abbot's Wood being incomplete. *The Times* of 6 October 1850 reported that,

> Trains from Worcester to Spetchley occupy exactly a quarter of an hour in the transit. The trains run up to the junction in about ten minutes and a brief delay is occasioned here by the shunting of the train on to the main line, but this accomplished, the run up to Spetchley is made in five minutes. There further delay is occasioned so that at present there is little saving of time by the opening of the branch, though the improvement as regards comfort [compared with the horse bus] is unquestionable. There is no huddling of fifteen persons in one lumbering conveyance for an hour's tedious jolting.

On 18 February 1852 the branch was continued northwards to Droitwich and Stoke Works Junction to complete the deviation line. MR passenger services eventually all ran via the deviation through Worcester until 1880 when all through services avoided the city, but stopping services still called.

The exterior of the Midland terminus at Gloucester, which closed 12 April 1896. (*Real Photographs*)

Chapter Eight

Accidents

In 1836, 0-2-2T *Surprise,* designed by Dr William Church of Birmingham, was built for Samuel Aspinall Goddard. Rather a curiosity, it had a vertical boiler and its footplate was at the front between the two cyclinders, the crew having no protection from the weather. It had been tried by the London & Birmingham and the Grand Junction companies and had languished for quite a time on a siding in Birmingham; so long, in fact, that rain had entered through the uncapped chimney and rusted away some of the boiler plating. On 3 November, the BGR agreed to find the fuel for a month's test. On the evening of 10 November, after making several short trips, it lived up to its name when the thin boiler plates burst with a tremendous explosion, killing Driver Thomas Scaife and injuring Joseph Rutherford, locomotive foreman, so badly that he died the next day. Their remains were interred in the churchyard of St John's, Bromsgrove, some 1½ miles west of the incline.

The stonemason was given the only available picture to work from, and as this depicted a Norris engine, an erroneous impression was given that an American engine had exploded. The painted tombstones are prominent to the south of the church. Rutherford left a widow and three small children, so, 'A spirited subscription has been commenced among the men at the station, (in which some officers have joined), in order if possible to put the poor woman in some small way of kindness in shopkeeping to which she has been somewhat accustomed, and by which it is hoped she may procure a living.' This incident was the very first boiler explosion report from a railway company received by the Railway Inspectorate.

At the inquest, it was revealed that Horton, the boiler maker, carried out work to Church's instructions, but Church had ordered the boiler plate too thin and it had a short life. John Riley, foreman to Horton, said that when Dr Church examined the work he was pleased, remarking, 'It is the best boiler I have seen in my life.' The boiler was proved in Horton's yard with a very high hydraulic pressure in the presence of Dr Church. Under Horton's direction, for safety, two of the plates exposed to the fire had been made ⅜ inch thick rather than the ¼ inch ordered by Church. The coroner imposed a deodand of £60 on the engine.

Repaired and renamed *Eclipse,* the engine was offered to the BGR for trial on 30 August 1842, but not surprisingly, the proposal was declined. On 25 January

Above left: Thomas Scaife's gravestone at St John's church, Bromsgrove, 4 June 1983. (*Author*)

Above right: Joseph Rutherford's vandalised gravestone at St John's church, Bromsgrove, 4 June 1983. (*Author*)

1844 the offer was repeated and this time accepted, but no record of the result has survived. In 1850 the locomotive stood at Camp Hill station, subsequently being bought by a colliery owner near Swansea. In 1857 it was dismantled in the workshops of the Swansea Vale Railway, the lengthened boiler being utilised in a new small-wheel 0-6-0T designed for hauling heavy mineral trains on sharply curved tracks. It came into Midland Railway hands when the company was taken over in 1874.

On 1 September 1840, the Up and Down Mails collided near Ashchurch and several passengers were injured.

On 7 April 1841 the locomotive superintendent, Creuze, and his foreman, Walworth, were drinking in a public house at Vigo Bank about two-thirds of the way up the incline, the bank engine of the last train having been ordered to wait for them. This locomotive had been modified by a tube being withdrawn so that a washout plug could be screwed into its hole in the front tube sheet, and when not in use, the gap in the firebox tube sheet was closed with a plain plug. As the

Norris 4-2-0 *William Gwynn* descended, the plug blew out, seriously scalding the driver, fireman and a switchman. Creuze, fatally injured, died the next day. Mrs Walworth, who had come to fetch her husband, and Tovey, a Nasmyth fitter, escaped with a shaking. It was revealed that Creuze was frequently intoxicated. On 9 April, Moorsom offered Herbert Spencer the office of assistant locomotive superintendent in place of G. D. Bishopp, who had been promoted to Creuze's post, but Spencer declined.

No less than two accidents occurred on Boxing Day 1840 on the 8.00 a.m. Gloucester to Birmingham. Soon after leaving Spetchley, one of the bogie wheels of the Norris engine broke, fortunately before much speed had been reached, the fireman and driver jumping to safety. Another Norris was coupled to the train and within a few hundred yards of Camp Hill station, firebars and fire fell on to the track. After a delay of some hours, the train was hauled to Camp Hill by a gang of between forty and fifty men. Two days later, the bogie wheels of another Norris broke, causing an accident.

On the evening of 20 January 1841, the last Down train from Birmingham to Gloucester hit an obstruction in the dark at Bredon Cutting. The engine left the road and began to climb the 40-foot-high slope. Driver Joseph Newport shut off steam and the engine stopped, embedded in the soil. Fortunately, the coupling between the tender and the first coach snapped, thus preventing the coaches from being derailed by the engine. Fireman Joseph Billingham, standing with one foot on the engine and the other on the tender at the time of derailment, unfortunately lost his balance and fell into a sitting position between the footplate of the tender and the footplate of the engine. Impetus drove the footplates together, nearly cutting off his legs at the knees. Mr Tate, a surgeon of Tewkesbury, was sent for and on arrival recommended that Billingham be taken to Gloucester Infirmary as soon as possible. There was a delay of one and a half hours while an engine was being sent from Gloucester. He was placed in a coach and conveyed to Gloucester, but was too weak to have an operation and died thirty minutes after being admitted. Sixteen men were required to free the engine from the cutting. Only its handrails were damaged. The inquest brought in a verdict of accidental death with a deodand of £20 on the engine.

The mishap was caused by the Down line being covered with 10 tons of ballast, 6 inches deep, brought down by a sudden frost after rain. Messrs Berwick & Lamb, who held the contract for maintaining the embankments, were engaged in removing the pile of gravel but had not completed the task by the time work was over for the day. The slip occurred only a few minutes before the train's arrival and in the darkness the driver had been unable to see the obstruction. Apart from the fireman, there were no injuries; no passenger was even jerked from his seat. The engine was re-railed during the night.

In February 1841, vandalism seems to have been at work for the BGR directors, who offered a £50 reward for the discovery of perpertratons of 'the late diabolical attempt to overset the trains'.

On 9 March 1841, just before dusk, James Howell, a labourer, was near Norton. Seeing a hammer on the rails in front of an approaching train, he sprang to remove it but was struck in the chest by a buffer. He died in Worcester Infirmary the next morning.

On 13 April 1842, one of the contractor's servants, George Barrick, neglected to alter the points near Gloucester station after the arrival of a goods train between 1.00 and 2.00 p.m. This resulted in the engine of the Down train being derailed, dragging off the tender and two coaches. F. H. P. Wetherall, the local railway superintendent, laid information on oath against Barrick for an offence against the byelaws and Barrick was fined £10, including expenses.

Sometimes it was the case of familiarity breeding contempt. On 27 April 1841 as the 6.00 p.m. train was approaching Eckington, Guard James Dudley was moving from the last coach, where he often sat unofficially, to his proper seat outside and while moving from one carriage to another, fell under the wheels and met instant death. William Stock was another guard who met with a fatal accident. He was sat on the roof chatting to a labourer when, approaching Barnt Green, the driver whistled for the brakes. Stock jumped up to apply the brakes at the instant the train passed under a bridge. He died in hospital.

On 2 July 1842 between Defford and Eckington, the driver of a Down goods noticed a wagon on fire. Instead of stopping and uncoupling it, he accelerated. The flames spread and in a few minutes the train presented 'the appearance of a moving mountain of fire'. Four wagons were alight and 'consumed down to their very axles'. All were Grand Junction Railway wagons laden with goods from Manchester, and the loss was estimated at between £600 and £800.

In June 1842 George Musto, pointsman at Eckington, fell asleep through drink, with the result that the Mail chopped off a leg. His replacement next evening was James Playdon who also fell asleep through drink. When the Mail arrived, he could not be found. He was eventually discovered, and received two months' hard labour for deserting his post.

In July 1843, McConnell and two fellow officers drove a train from Gloucester to Tewkesbury races. As it approached Tewkesbury, McConnell found he was unable to stop, the probable cause being priming. The *Railway Record* continues:

> At the top end [of the station] there is a gateway and beyond that a line of rails which crosses a public street and leads down to the river. There was some scaffolding erected inside this gateway which would not admit of an engine to pass under it but on this occasion the engine proceeded at full speed under the gateway, the scaffolding catching the chimney bringing it down. The engine getting into the street killed a passing pig. The engine and train kept bending their way to the River Avon and had it not been from chance, those most perfect of enginemen and their superior officer would have had a cooling dip in the river.

A similar event happened in November 1846 when an engine and coach smashed through the station house doors at Tewkesbury before crossing High Street and proceeding down Quay Lane, stopping before it plunged into the river.

On 8 April 1845, as the Up train that had left Cheltenham at 3.30 p.m. was within a mile of Ashchurch station and proceeding at about 25 mph when 'it was discovered that the engine had lost three wheels, and had it not been for an extra wheel lately added and its large wheels, the destruction of the train would have been certain. An explosion of the boiler took place, and in a few moments the flames communicated to the luggage van. Fortunately assistance was at hand, and by means of the breaks (*sic*) the train was stopped without any great shock. The engineer and stoker escaped without injury, by clinging to the rails. The confusion among the passengers was great, but fortunately no one received any injury.'

On 26 June, the 10.30 a.m. from Gloucester was approaching Camp Hill when it crashed head-on into a Down goods train, single line working being in force at the time. The engine of the Up train was completely destroyed, Driver Cole and his fireman being badly injured as they jumped to safety. The other engine was seriously damaged. The accident was caused through the Down train leaving Birmingham contrary to orders. The company did everything it possibly could for the injured; a man who was seriously injured had a train sent to collect his relatives.

In July 1845, a permanent way labourer sat down near the line to eat lunch and have a nap. A train went by and he was feared killed, but the wheels had merely passed along his side and legs, cutting the material of his clothes, but only grazing him.

The worst accident to date was on 30 August 1845 at about 10.15 p.m. Goods wagons had been left on the Up line about 30 yards north of Defford station, ready to be coupled to the Down third-class train, which left Birmingham at 7.30 p.m.

At Defford, the signal was against the 9.00 p.m. twenty-wagon Up goods train from Gloucester, eighteen wagons of which were loaded with iron rails and timber drawn by MR 0-6-0 No. 75 only built the previous year, but Driver Joseph Ward, noted for his recklessness, ignored it, continued on at 30 mph and struck the wagon, thrusting it to the Down line. The impact drove his engine across both roads, its tender pushed up the side of the cutting. Ward was killed, and his fireman, James Baird, escaped death but was very badly injured and taken to Gloucester Infirmary.

Although it was dark, Joseph Pickering, driver of the 7.45 p.m. passenger train from Birmingham to Gloucester, spotted the obstruction, closed the regulator and reversed. He and fireman Benjamin Giles leaped off just before it struck the goods engine. It dragged the first coach on top of the goods engine, whereupon the coach ignited; the following coach was smashed to pieces. The *Bristol Times* commented, 'The passengers, mostly of the poorer class, were thrown in all directions.' One such passenger, William Miles, a carpenter from Cheltenham employed by the contractors, cut, bruised and scalded, died within a few hours. Until this accident, no BGR passenger had lost their life.

Passengers were delayed for four and a half hours as they had to wait until a locomotive and coaches could be sent from Gloucester. The empty coaching stock sent to collect them carried the superintendents of Gloucester and Cheltenham station and also workmen to clear the debris. Railway officials estmiated the cost of the damage at £3,000–£5,000. It was questionable wisdom that stationmaster James Dore should have placed a wagon on a main line just before two trains were due. Dore also refused to asssist the badly injured fireman and left Ward's body in a barn for two days, covered with empty coke sacks.

At the inquest, fireman Baird explained that at Bredon he experienced a faulty water pump and while attending to this, the fire became low. By Eckington, the pumps were working correctly and Ward said he would assist with the fire, opening and closing the firebox door when Baird put on coke. Near Defford, Ward exclaimed, 'Jamie, there's something wrong!' and shut off steam, while Baird threw the engine into reverse, but while doing so, he was thrown off and knocked unconscious. Helpers revived him by pouring water. The jury was locked up for nearly four hours before bringing in a verdict of accidental death and awarding a deodand of £1,500 (its value) against the engine. No. 75 was repaired and eventually broken up in May 1866.

On 26 November 1891, the Up Night Mail, which left Bristol for Derby at 1.03 a.m., ran into a goods train at Barnt Green. Fortunately, there were less than ten passengers on the train and their coach was separated from the engine by a van and empty cattle truck, these vehicles bearing the brunt of the collision. The line was cleared by noon.

On 26 October 1893, the 1.25 p.m. Bristol to Birmingham ran into six wagons left on the line at Stoke Works Junction, injuring five passengers. A goods train had left six wagons on the Up main line when it moved to the Worcester branch to allow the express to pass. The foreman shunter failed to see that the wagons were coupled to the train and the goods guard ought to have been aware that almost a third of his train was missing. The passenger train driver observed the wagons ahead, but being on a curve, did not appreciate that they were on his road until he was 50 yards away. The first wagon was smashed to pieces, derailing the engine across the Down line, while the other five were propelled a quarter of a mile along the track.

On 26 September 1899, when the Ashchurch to Malvern train was being shunted from the main to the branch line at Ashchurch, the engine derailed at points and heeled over on its side, the coaches following. Guard Lane was hurled against the brake handle in his van and several ribs were broken. The driver and fireman jumped to safety.

The line was mercifully free of incidents until 27 November 1921. The 4.12 a.m. for Tamworth, delayed at New Street by engine trouble, was struck by an express from Bristol Temple Meads, which had run through signals. Ticket Inspector Barrington foresaw the danger and shouted a warning through the compartment windows allowing some passengers to escape, but three on the Tamworth train were killed and fourteen injured. The accident occurred through the express driver mishearing the fireman saying the signal was 'Off' when he actually called 'On'.

On 23 February 1924 when the 9.10 p.m. Bath to Birmingham freight consisting of 0-6-0 No. 3071, eight loaded wagons and forty empties, arrived at Stoke Works Junction. The signalman, knowing that the 1.10 a.m. ex-Bristol Up Mail was near, decided to shunt the goods from the Up to the Down line in order to let the Mail overtake. The goods was duly moved from the Up to the Down road and the fireman correctly changed his engine's headlamps from white to red.

2-4-0 No. 175 and an inspection saloon at the site of the Ashchurch accident, 8 January 1929. (*Author's collection*)

Meanwhile, the 2.50 a.m. Birmingham to Bristol passenger and mail consisting of 4-4-0 No. 395 with a load of four coaches, five vans and three post office tenders was approaching. Driver Bent saw that the distant signal was clear, but as he approached the junction, saw red lights on an engine and his home signal thrown to red. Fortunately only travelling at 20 mph due to the turnout, he immediately braked but was struck by the goods engine at about 12 mph, bruising fifteen GPO officials.

On 8 January 1929, the driver of 4-4-0 Midland Compound No. 1060, hauling a load of ten bogie coaches and four six-wheelers on the 7.20 p.m. Bristol to Nottingham approaching Ashchurch Junction, overran his signals which were enveloped in sudden fog and crashed at 50 mph into a goods train with 0-6-0 No. 3562, setting back over a trailing crossover from the Up to the Down line. Unlike a similar disaster at Charfield 34 miles to the south and less than three months before, although a small fire started, fortunately it was quickly doused by water from a hydrant at the station. All the passenger coaches were electrically lit, but the mail vehicles were illuminated by gas. The pipes fractured and gas escaped, 'filling the coaches almost to suffocation point' (*Bristol Times*). Luckily the train was only carrying forty-five passengers so the death toll was light – two passengers, the mail train driver and a fireman returning 'on the cushions'. It was ironic that J. Lowes, the fireman who was killed, was to have fired the Mail, but was unwell and at Gloucester asked for relief. Fireman Cleverley took his place on the footplate and lived, only suffering minor injuries. Twenty-one injured passengers were taken to hospital at Tewkesbury by ambulance and private car.

Guard Moulton of Derby was sorting parcels when the collision took place. The bottom of his van opened and he found himself lying in a field with a broken arm. Despite his injuries, by scrambling up the splintered woodwork using one arm he brought eight passengers from a coach thrown 30 feet into the air. He assisted in freeing the trapped passengers through doors and windows, passing them to post office officials below. Not until the last passenger had been brought out would he allow himself to be treated. Some of the post office staff on the train had been involved in the Charfield accident.

Ashchurch was also the scene of an accident on 8 March 1969. Class 47 D1754 was working the 07.50 Washwood Heath to Stoke Gifford consisting of fifty-seven loaded wagons. South of the station, the twelfth wagon, a 16-ton mineral wagon loaded with coal, derailed and struck coaches of the passing 10.40 Bristol to Newcastle consisting of eleven coaches hauled by Class 45 D156. Damage to the passenger train was confined to the sixth to eleventh coaches. Twelve ambulances conveyed forty-three passengers and four railway staff to hospitals at Cheltenham and Tewkesbury. One passenger was dead on arrival and another died the following day. Breakdown cranes arrived from Saltley, Bristol and Swindon and the line was cleared by 19.00 on 9 March.

Major C. F. Rose found that the accident was caused by excessive speed. The goods train was restricted to 35 mph due to a heavy, loaded bogie wagon towards the rear, but the speed was probably over 45 mph. Twists in the track in excess of tolerances laid down for a main line contributed to the disaster.

A scheme for promoting the Cross-City line is advertised on this May 1978 poster. (*British Railways*)

Chapter Nine

Train Services

The opening service from Cheltenham to Bromsgrove on 24 June 1840 showed two trains each way and none on Sundays. A road connection was made between Bromsgrove and Birmingham. Two night mails commenced on 6 February 1841, 'but owing to the unreasonableness of the hours, the number of passengers conveyed by these trains has been very small.' Cheltenham strictly observed the Sabbath. When the line was opened, great efforts were made to prevent Sunday trains being run other than the four mails ordered by the Post Office, the Reverend Francis Close appealing to the directors, other shareholders and later George Hudson. Close observed that as previously no road coaches had run on Sundays, this suggested that the public did not wish to travel on that day. Some shareholders wished to overrule the directors' decision, so a special meeting was held on 23 March 1841 to determine whether Sunday trains should be run. Forty-one voted against Sunday trains other than mails, thirty voted for two trains in each direction outside church service hours. Francis Close was successful in holding off Sunday trains until the passing of the Railways Act of 1846 enforced the running of certain passenger trains on the first day of the week.

On 3 May 1841, 623 members of the Gloucester Mechanics' Institute visited Birmingham by rail. At 6.30 a.m. the special left Gloucester, picking up members from Cheltenham and Ashchurch en route. It consisted of twenty-three coaches comprising five first-class, twelve second-class, and six third-class. It was drawn by two locomotives. As first-class coaches seated eighteen and those of second-class twenty-four, forty-six must have been packed into each third-class coach. At Bromsgrove the train was divided, the first fourteen coaches climbing the Lickey Incline with one of the train engines plus a banker. After a good start, the train stalled halfway up and had to be assisted in the rear by the banker of the second portion. The second half climbed successfully, but the delay meant they did not arrive at Birmingham until 10.30 a.m. Return was at 6.30 p.m.

Another similar excursion had twenty-two coaches, half of which were open third-class. It rained and apart from soaking the passengers, this affected the locomotives' adhesion to the extent that both legs of the journey took five hours instead of four. A thirteen-coach excursion in June 1843 left Gloucester for Liverpool and Bangor, and joined at Birmingham with one from Nottingham and Derby. The thirty-four coaches went to Liverpool and returned three days later.

First and second class carriages with all the trains. Third class carriages with trains Nos. 1 and 9 from Gloucester, and 8 and 11 from Birmingham.

Only the mail trains run on Sundays.

DAY TICKETS from Cheltenham to Gloucester,

First Class, 2s.

Second Class, 1s. 6d.

DOWN TRAINS

BIRMINGHAM										
Camp Hill										
Moseley										
Longbridge										
Barnt Green										
Blackwell										
BROMSGROVE										
Stoke Works										
DROITWICH										
Dunhampstead										
SPETCHLEY										
WORCESTER { arriv. / dep.										
Norton										
WADBOROUGH										
Besford										
Defford										
Bredon										
ASHCHURCH										
TEWKESBURY { arr / dp.										
Cleeve										
CHELTENHAM										
Badgworth										
GLOUCESTER .. arr.										

UP TRAINS.

Station											
DEPARTURE FROM											
GLOUCESTER											
Badgworth											
CHELTENHAM											
Cleeve											
ASHCHURCH											
TEWKESBURY { arr / dp.											
Bredon											
Eckington											
Defford											
Wadborough											
Norton											
SPETCHLEY											
WORCESTER { arriv. / dep.											
Dunhampstead											
DROITWICH											
Stoke Works											
BROMSGROVE											
Blackwell											
Barnt Green											
Longbridge											
Moseley											
Camp Hill											
BIRMINGHAM .. arr											

The BGR timetable from *Bradshaw's Railway Guide*, January 1845.

18 **Through Table.—Bristol and Exeter and Midland Railways.**

Miles from Exeter.	UP. These Classes refer to B. & E. Stations only.	WEEK DAYS.												Sundays.		
		A 1 2 P	1 2 3		1 2 3	1 2	A 1 2 P	1 2		1 2	Mail 1 2	1 2 3	Mail 1 2	1 2 P	1 2	Mail 1 2
		a.m	a.m		p.m.	a.m	a.m	p.m		p.m	p.m	p.m	p.m	a.m	p.m	p.m
	EXETER .. .. .. dep.	6 0	..	..	..	9 45	11 50	12 50	..	3 10	4 45	..	10 12	9 40	3 25	10 12
8¼	Hele and Bradninch ..	6 26	..	..	..	..	12 16	..	..	3 33	..	..	..	10 8	3 43	..
12¼	Cullompton	6 37	..	..	..	..	12 27	..	..	3 44	..	..	..	10 20	3 53	..
14¾	Tiverton Junction ..	6 45	..	..	..	10 15	12 35	..	..	3 52	..	..	..	10 29	4 1	..
19¾	Tiverton	..	..	..	..	9 55	12 20	..	..	3 37	..	..	..	10 14	3 44	..
19¼	Burlescombe	6 58	..	..	..	..	12 47	..	..	..	..	..	..	10 43	..	..
23¾	Wellington	7 11	..	..	..	10 35	12 59	..	..	4 8	..	..	..	10 57	4 19	..
	Minehead	..	..	..	..	8 10	11 20	11 20	..	1 55	..	..	..	..	..	..
1½	Dunster	..	..	..	..	8 16	11 26	11 26	..	2 1	..	..	..	..	..	..
8	Watchet	..	..	..	..	8 41	11 50	11 50	..	2 25	..	..	..	..	..	..
9½	Williton	..	..	..	..	8 49	11 57	11 57	..	2 32	..	..	..	..	..	..
	Chard	6 0	..	..	..	9 15	12 10	12 10	..	3 35	..	..	..	..	..	..
	Ilminster	6 26	..	..	..	9 25	12 20	12 20	..	3 45	..	..	..	..	..	..
Dev. & Som. Branch.	Ilfracombe, by coach	..	..	..	..	..	8 30	8 30	..	..	..	..	..	..	..	..
	Barnstaple	..	..	..	..	9 0	10 30	10 30	..	1 15	3 30	..	..	..	..	..
10½	South Molton	..	..	..	..	9 20	11 2	11 2	..	1 48	3 50	..	..	..	..	..
23½	Dulverton..	..	..	..	..	10 2	11 33	11 33	..	2 33	4 15	..	..	..	..	..
26½	Morebath, for Bmptn.	..	..	..	..	..	11 41	11 41	..	2 41	..	..	..	..	..	..
35½	Wiveliscombe	..	..	..	..	10 20	12 6	12 6	..	3 4	4 53	..	..	..	..	..
38	Milverton..	..	..	..	..	..	12 16	12 16	..	3 14	..	..	..	..	..	..
30¾	Taunton..	7 35	..	..	..	11 15	1 50	1 38	..	4 27	5 31	..	11 12	11 20	4 40	11 12
Yeovil Branch.	Weymouth	5 20	..	..	..	8 10	10 0	..	..	..	..	..	..	..	..	..
	Yeovil (Pen Mill) ..	6 10	..	..	..	9 25	11 40	..	..	3 45	..	..	..	..	..	..
7	Martock	6 33	..	..	..	9 50	11 55	..	..	4 0	..	..	..	..	..	..
12	Langport	6 47	..	..	..	10 2	12 11	..	..	4 12	..	..	..	..	..	..
19	Durston .. .. arr.	7 10	..	..	..	10 20	12 32	..	..	4 30	..	..	..	..	..	..
36¾	Durston .. .. .. dep.	7 49	..	..	..	11 31	2 6	..	..	4 40	..	..	..	11 35	4 54	..
42¼	Bridgwater	8 4	..	..	..	11 47	2 22	..	..	4 54	5 51	..	11 37	11 54	5 7	11 37
48½	Highbridge	8 24	..	..	..	12 3	2 45	..	..	5 8	..	..	..	12 12	5 21	..
57	Weston-s.-Mare Junc.	8 55	10 5	..	..	12 26	3 14	..	..	5 32	..	7 26	..	12 39	5 37	..
58½	Weston-s.-Mare ..	8 20	10 0	..	..	12 11	3 0	..	..	5 20	..	7 20	..	12 29	5 25	..
60	Worle	9 3	..	..	..	..	3 24	..	..	..	..	7 32	..	12 48	..	..
C. Valley Branch.	Wells..	7 45	..	..	..	..	2 20	..	..	..	..	..	..	..	..	..
8	Cheddar	8 13	..	..	..	..	2 48	..	..	..	..	..	..	..	..	..
9½	Axbridge	8 20	..	..	..	..	2 55	..	..	..	..	..	..	..	..	..
12	Winscombe	8 27	..	..	..	..	3 2	..	..	..	..	..	..	..	..	..
13	Sandford & Banwell	8 32	..	..	..	..	3 7	..	..	..	..	..	..	..	..	..
63¼	Yatton	9 13	10 17	..	12 12	..	3 35	..	..	5 47	..	7 40	..	12 56	5 49	..
67½	Clevedon	8 45	10 3	..	12 0	..	3 10	..	..	5 27	..	..	..	12 44	5 35	..
67½	Nailsea	9 21	..	..	12 22	..	3 45	..	..	..	..	..	..	1 5	5 59	..
70	Bourton	9 30	10 32	..	12 30	..	3 55	..	..	..	..	..	..	..	..	..
75¼	BRISTOL .. .. .. arr.	9 50	10 40	..	12 45	1 5	4 15	2 50	..	6 15	6 45	8 5	12 32	1 30	6 20	12 32
		F 1 & 3	1 & 3		F 1 & 3		1 & 2	F 1 & 3		1 & 3			1 & 3	1 & 3	1 & 3	1 & 3
		a.m	a.m.		p.m		p.m	p.m		p.m			a.m	p.m	p.m	a.m
	BRISTOL .. .. .. dep.	10 15	11 0	..	1 20		5 0	3 20	..	7 0		..	12 45	4 50	7 0	12 45
86	Yate .. .. .. arr.	..	11 33	..	1 47		5 27	..	..	7 57		..	..	5 20	..	..
97¾	Berkeley Road	..	12 1	..	2 9		5 43	4 3	..	7 41		..	..	5 47	7 41	..
104	Stonehouse	..	12 20	..	2 20		6 12	..	..	7 51		..	1 39	6 3	7 51	1 39
113	GLO'STER .. { arr.	11 20	12 42	..	2 40		6 35	4 30	..	8 13		..	2 0	6 25	8 13	2 0
	{ dep.	11 30	12 50	..	2 51		6 45	4 40	..	8 23		..	8 0	6 35	8 23	7 35
120	Cheltenham .. .. arr.	11 42	1 5	..	3 3		7 0	4 52	..	8 34		..	8 15	6 48	8 34	7 47
129	Tewkesbury	..	1 36	..	4 30		7 40	5 26	..	9 0		..	8 57	..	..	..
	Great Malvern	..	2 10	..	..		8 15	5 57	..	..		..	..	..	..	..
142	WORCESTER	12 20	2 3	..	3 41		8 9	5 35	..	9 16		..	9 24	7 55	9 16	8 48
153½	Bromsgrove	12 44	2 45	..	4 8		8 43	6 0	..	9 39		..	9 55	8 30	9 39	9 22
169½	BIRMINGHAM (New St.)	1 23	3 35	..	4 50		9 48	6 40	..	10 18		..	11 0	9 40	10 18	10 20
	Leicester	4 0	..	..	6 17		..	8 5	..	1 44		..	12 32	..	1 44	..
188	Tamworth	1 58	4 54	..	5 31		..	7 17	..	11 51		..	..	..	11 51	..
201	Burton J. for Lcs. & N. S.	2 22	5 27	..	5 53		..	7 38	..	11 22		..	12 27	..	12 16	..
212	DERBY .. .. .. arr.	2 45	5 55	..	6 15		..	8 0	..	11 45		..	12 50	..	12 38	..
	Buxton, v. Matlock arr.	4 40	7 40	..	8 10		..	..	..	..		..	..	..	..	..
	Manchester, v. Matlock	5 0	..	..	8 10		..	9 45	..	5 10		..	2 50	..	..	..
	Liverpool (Ranelagh St.)	6 0	..	..	9 0		..	10 35	..	6 0		..	3 45	..	..	..
227½	Nottingham	3 45	7 5	..	7 15		..	9 15	..	1 30		..	1 50	..	1 30	..
257½	Sheffield..	4 1	..	..	7 46		..	10 5	..	12 46		..	1 58	..	1 41	..
	Hull	8 0	..	..	11 15		..	..	..	4 33		..	5 42	..	4 32	..
	York	6 50	..	..	10 20		..	..	..	3 36		..	4 30	..	3 36	..
	Scarborough	9 20	..	..	..		..	..	..	5 45		..	7 0	..	5 45	..
	Newcastle	11 20	..	..	12 45		..	..	..	5 53		..	7 45	..	5 58	..
286	Leeds	5 25	..	..	9 20		..	..	..	2 2		..	3 25	..	3 0	..
	Bradford..	8 10	..	..	9 50		..	..	..	2 45		..	3 0	..	3 55	..
	Carlisle	..	..	..	..		..	..	..	5 4		..	6 25	..	..	..
	Edinburgh, Wvly. Bdg.	..	..	..	..		..	..	..	7 35		..	8 55	..	..	..
	GLASGOW, St. Enoch ..	..	..	..	..		..	..	..	8 0		..	9 20	..	..	..

For **REFERENCE NOTES** see page 26.

A timetable showing through trains in January 1877 between the MR at Birmingham New Street and the Bristol & Exeter Railway at Exeter.

Through Table.—Bristol and Exeter and Midland Railways. 19

Miles from Derby.	DOWN.	Week Days p.m	Week Days ¶ ¶ p.m	¶ ¶ Monday mornings excepted			G p.m	G a.m	G a.m	G a.m	Sundays.	Sundays p.m	Sundays
	GLASGOW, St. Enoch dp.	10 15	4 35		..	..	9 15	..	..	..	..	4 35	..
	Edinburgh, Wvly. Bdg.	10 25	4 30		..	..	9 20	..	..	..	..	4 30	..
	Carlisle	1 10	8 10		..	..	12 10	..	..	8 25	..	8 10	..
	Bradford..	3 55	10 25		..	..	2 15	..	8 0	12 30	..	10 25	..
	Leeds	4 20	11 30		..	..	3 20	..	8 50	1 20	..	11 30	..
	Newcastle	..	7 8		..	..	11 23	..	2 5	10 5	..	7 8	..
	Scarborough	11 0	7 0		..	..	..	..	8 15	11 0	..	7 0	..
	York	3 25	9 38		..	..	2 10	..	6 50	12 50	..	9 38	..
	Hull	..	8 50		..	..	..	..	5 45	10 30	..	8 50	..
	Sheffield..	5 35	12 34		..	..	4 30	7 0	10 10	2 28	..	12 34	..
	Nottingham	5 45	11 40		..	..	..	7 45	10 50	2 35	..	11 40	..
	Liverpool (Ranelagh St.)	4 0	10 40		..	..	..	..	9 0	12 0	..	10 40	..
	Manchester via Matlock	4 50	11 30		..	..	..	7 0	9 50	1 0	..	11 30	..
	Buxton, via Matlock ..	3 50	7 5		..	..	..	..	10 20	1 30	..	..	..
	DERBY .. .. .. dep.	6 50	1 45	..	..	..	6 45	8 40	11 35	3 40	..	1 45	..
11	Burton J. for Les. & N.S.	7 10	2 3	..	..	..	7 15	9 2	11 56	3 58	..	2 3	..
24	Tamworth	7 33	2 26	..	..	..	7 49	9 24	11 22	4 20	..	2 26	..
	Leicester	6 45	11 42	..	..	..	..	8 15	..	2 55	..	11 42	..

Miles		1 & 3 p.m	1 & 3 a.m	1 & 3 a m	1 & 3 a.m	1 & 3 a.m	1 & 3 a.m	1 & 3 p.m	1 & 3 p.m	Sundays 1 & 3 p.m	Sundays 1 & 3 a.m	Sundays 1 & 3 a.m
	BIRMINGHAM (New St.)	8 10	2 45	..	6 40	8 45	10 5	12 40	4 45	4 35	2 45	..
58½	Bromsgrove	8 55	..	..	7 44	9 20	10 51	1 14	5 27	5 30	..	..
70	WORCESTER	9 29	4 2	..	8 33	9 49	11 25	1 46	5 55	6 6	4 2	..
	Great Malvern	6 30	..	..	8 25	..	11 7	..	..	..	..	..
87	Tewkesbury	7 5	..	..	9 0	10 0	11 42	..	6 5	..	..	..
92	Cheltenham	10 7	4 33	..	9 31	10 28	12 13	2 19	6 31	7 2	4 33	..
99	GLO'STER .. .. arr.	10 30	4 53	..	9 53	10 45	12 33	2 38	6 50	7 23	4 53	..
	GLO'STER dep.	11 15	5 0	8 10	10 0	10 52	12 40	2 45	6 57	11 15	5 0	8 40
108	Stonehouse	11 30	..	8 30	10 20	..	1 0	..	..	11 30	..	9 1
114½	Berkeley Road	..	..	8 47	10 37	..	1 14	..	..	8 6	..	9 16
126	Yate	..	..	9 13	11 6	..	1 38	..	..	8 31	..	9 41
136½	BRISTOL .. .. .. arr.	12 20	6 0	9 40	11 35	11 55	2 10	3 50	8 0	12 20	6 0	10 15

Miles	These Classes refer to B. & E. Stations only.	Mail 1 2 a.m	Mail 1 2 a.m	1 2 3 a.m	1 2 P a.m	1 2 3 a.m	B 1 2 p.m	B 1 2 3 p.m	Exp 1 2 p.m	B 1 2 p.m	B 1 2 P p.m	1 2 p.m	1 2 P p.m	Sundays Mail 1 2 a.m	Sundays 1 2 P a.m	Sundays 1 2 p.m
	BRISTOL .. .. .. dep.	12 30	6 15	10 50	11 0	11 50	12 10	12 40	2 26	3 15	4 40	8 15	8 50	12 30	6 30	3 30
	Bourton .. .. .. arr.	..	..	..	11 16	..	..	..	..	..	4 56	..	9 3	..	..	..
144½	Nailsea	..	..	..	11 25	..	..	..	..	3 35	5 4	..	9 10	..	6 48	3 43
148½	Yatton	..	..	11 15	11 36	12 14	..	1 5	..	3 47	5 14	..	9 20	..	6 59	3 59
152½	Clovedon	..	..	11 30	..	..	..	..		4 15	5 25	..	9 45	..	7 10	4 15
C. Valley Branch.	Sandford & Banwell	..	..	11 57	11 57	..	..	1 23	¶ Slip Carriage detached at 3.6 p.m	4 13	..	..	..	..	..	..
1	Winscombe	..	..	12 2	12 2	..	..	1 28		4 18	..	..	..	..	..	..
3½	Axbridge	..	..	12 8	11 8	..	..	1 35		4 25	..	..	..	..	..	..
5	Cheddar	..	..	12 14	12 14	..	..	1 42		4 32	..	..	..	..	..	..
13	Wells	..	..	12 45	12 45	..	..	2 10		5 0	..	..	..	..	..	..
152	Worle	..	..	..	11 46	..	..	1 13		4 0	..	..	9 28	..	7 8	4 8
155	Weston-s.-Mare Junc.	..	6 43	11 30	11 56	12 30	12 48	1 19		4 11	..	Slip	9 38	..	7 17	4 17
156½	Weston-s.-Mare ..	..	6 58	11 40	12 2	12 35	1 0	1 34		4 21	..	8 50	9 45	..	7 27	4 30
163½	Highbridge	..	6 58	11 47	..	..	..	1 45	..	4 42	..	8 51	..	..	7 34	4 34
169½	Bridgwater	1 23	7 11	11 59	..	..	1 12	2 5	¶	5 0	..	9 6	..	1 23	7 49	4 49
175½	Durston	..	7 24	12 13	..	..	1 26	2 20	..	5 15	..	..	..	..	8 3	5 3
Yeovil Branch.	Durston .. .. Dep.	..	8 0	..	..	..	1 55	..	..	5 25	..	..	..	..	..	..
7	Langport .. .. Arr	..	8 23	..	..	..	2 22	..	..	5 49	..	..	..	..	..	..
12	Martock	..	8 41	..	..	..	2 32	..	..	5 59	..	..	..	..	..	..
19	Yeovil (Pen Mill) ..	..	9 0	..	..	..	2 50	..	..	6 20	..	..	..	..	..	..
	Weymouth	..	10 40	..	..	..	4 0	..	..	10 35	..	..	..	..	..	..
181¼	Taunton	1 48	7 37	12 30	..	..	1 10	2 38	3 18	5 30	..	9 24	..	1 48	8 18	5 23
Dev. & Som. Branch.	Milverton	..	8 5	..	..	..	1 51	..	3 47	6 2	..	..	..	..	..	..
3	Wiveliscombe	..	8 15	..	..	..	2 1	..	3 58	6 13	..	..	..	..	..	..
11½	Morebath, for Bmptn.	..	8 40	..	..	..	2 23	..	..	6 36	..	..	..	..	..	..
14¾	Dulverton	..	8 52	..	..	..	2 33	..	4 32	6 50	..	..	..	..	..	..
28	South Molton	..	9 42	..	..	..	2 55	..	5 0	7 29	..	..	..	..	..	..
38½	Barnstaple	..	10 12	..	..	..	3 23	..	5 20	8 0	..	..	..	..	..	..
	Ilfracombe, by coach	..	..	..	..	..	..	..	7 15	..	..	..	..	..	..	..
	Ilminster	..	8 30	..	..	..	2 41	..	..	6 20	..	..	..	..	..	..
4	Chard..	..	8 50	..	..	..	2 55	..	..	6 40	..	..	..	..	..	..
	Williton	..	8 49	..	..	..	2 32	..	..	6 32	..	..	..	..	..	..
1¼	Watchet	..	8 50	..	..	..	2 40	..	..	6 40	..	..	..	..	..	..
8	Dunster	..	9 24	..	..	..	3 5	..	..	7 5	..	..	..	..	..	..
9¾	Minehead	..	9 29	..	..	..	3 10	..	..	7 10	..	..	..	..	..	..
188¼	Wellington	..	..	..	..	..	2 4	..	3 54	5 56	..	..	..	..	8 34	5 39
192¾	Burlescombe	..	..	..	..	..	2 19	..	4 5	..	..	..	..	..	..	5 52
197¼	Tiverton Junction ..	..	8 7	..	..	..	2 29	..	4 16	6 17	..	9 57	..	..	8 54	6 3
202¼	Tiverton	..	8 22	..	..	..	2 44	..	4 30	6 35	..	10 10	..	..	9 9	6 20
199¼	Cullompton	..	..	..	..	..	2 37	..	4 24	6 25	..	..	..	..	9 1	6 10
203¾	Hele and Bradninch ..	..	..	..	..	..	2 47	..	4 34	6 33	..	..	..	..	9 10	6 20
212	EXETER	2 50	8 27	..	..	..	2 10	..	4 0	7 0	..	10 20	..	2 50	9 35	6 45

For REFERENCE NOTES see page 26.

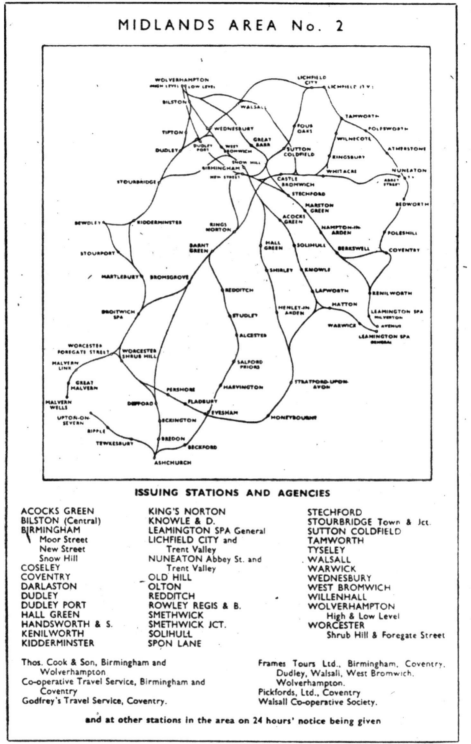

Handbill dated June 1956 advertising that the Birmingham to Ashchurch section of line could be covered on a Holiday Runabout Ticket.

HOLIDAY RUNABOUT
TICKETS

IN

THE MIDLANDS

DURING

INDUSTRIAL and AUGUST
HOLIDAY WEEKS

29th July—11th August 1956

EACH AREA

Second 25/- Class

(Children under fourteen—half-fare)

- TICKETS AVAILABLE 7 DAYS SUNDAY TO SATURDAY (inclusive)
- UNLIMITED NUMBER OF JOURNEYS WITHIN THE AREA
- BREAK OF JOURNEY ALLOWED AT ANY STATION
- TAKE YOUR BICYCLE FOR 12/6
- TAKE YOUR DOG FOR 6/3

These tickets are issued subject to the British Transport Commission's published Regulations and Conditions applicable to British Railways exhibited at their stations, or obtainable free of charge at Station Booking Office.

Further information will be supplied on application to Stations, Official Railway Agents or to G. F. Luther, District Passenger Manager, London Midland and Western Regions. New Street Station, Birmingham 2. Telephone MIDland 2740 ; H. Bullough, District Commercial Manager, London Road, Leicester, Telephone 5542 ; C. E. Drew, District Commercial Manager, Shrub Hill Station. Worcester, Telephone 3241.

June, 1956   B.R. 35008/1

For their outing in 1844, the Gloucester Mechanics' Institute travelled to Bristol on 15 July. Two trains were run, one from Gloucester and the other from Worcester, Tewkesbury, and Cheltenham. The Gloucester contingent fared well, the others less so. Their train was late leaving Bristol and treated abominably by BGR staff at Gloucester and Cheltenham. A Worcester passenger complained that, 'On returning, a delay of two hours took place at the Gloucester Station and upon some parties naturally becoming a little clamourous to ascertain the cause of delay, some man in authority called out: "If those fellows don't keep quiet, keep them locked in another half hour."'

On arrival at Cheltenham, around forty first-class passengers, who had been told that their coach would run through, were unceremoniously turned out by the superintendent there and it was not until they had been kept in the cold until nearly 1.00 a.m. that he provided other coaches. The only answer the passengers could obtain from him was that, 'If they did not like it, they should not have gone.' Instead of arriving at Worcester at 11.00 p.m. they did not do so until 3.00 a.m.

A junction was made with the London & Birmingham Railway on 17 August 1841 and to cope with the expected additional traffic, two trains were added to run over the whole of the BGR and the four short workings from Cheltenham to Gloucester discontinued. Fares Gloucester to Birmingham were: first class 13s 6d, second class 9s 0d and third class 5s 6d. In 1843, arrangements were made with the Birmingham & Derby to run through coaches by two trains each way daily. From 14 November 1842 it was agreed with the London & Birmingham to run a through first-class coach from Euston to Gloucester, the 9.45 a.m. ex-Euston was due Gloucester at 5.15 p.m., while the 1.00 p.m. ex-Gloucester was due Euston at 9.00 p.m. It was the only rail route available from Gloucester to London, the Bristol & Gloucester Railway and the Cheltenham & Great Western Union Railway not being opened until 1844. The journey time of seven and a half hours included forty minutes for transfer of coaches at Curzon Street. In August 1843, four short working trains were reinstated between Cheltenham and Gloucester. On 1 March 1847, eight trains ran each way daily between Gloucester and Birmingham and three on Sundays, the fastest covering the distance of 50 miles in one hour fifty minutes.

In January 1877, seven trains ran each way and three on Sundays, the fastest taking two hours. In August 1877 timetables showed eleven Down (five on Sundays), the fastest covering the distance in one hour twenty-one minutes; in the reverse direction there were eleven Up (four on Sundays), the fastest taking one hour twenty-nine minutes. In 1880 the MR inaugurated through trains from the North to Bournemouth via Bath and the Somerset & Dorset Railway. These were coaches attached to Bristol expresses from Bradford and later Newcastle, being detached at Mangotsfield. In 1888, a through coach was introduced from Bradford to Plymouth via the S&D and LSWR at Templecombe. The total time of the stops was fifty-two minutes and it kept up a steady 45–48 mph average from station to station. Between Derby and Bristol it was worked by a 7-foot 6-inch single. The April 1910 Bradshaw showed thirteen Down trains between Birmingham and Gloucester (six on Sundays), the fastest taking one hour thirty minutes, while in the reverse direction there were nineteen Up (eight on Sundays), the fastest taking one hour ten minutes.

The first through train between Manchester and Bournemouth via Birmingham and Bath was introduced on 1 October 1910. It worked over LNWR metals from Manchester to Birmingham and to avoid reversal at New Street, went via Camp Hill to King's Norton. It received the name Pines Express in 1927. The northbound Pines Express travelled via Selly Oak, which meant that it passed through New Street in the same direction as the southbound Pines, even using the same platform. It made its last run on 8 September 1962 before being rerouted via Snow Hill and Oxford. The Devonian, also named in 1927, ran from Bradford to Paignton, although only three coaches made the whole trip, the rest terminating at Bristol. In 1952 the Cornishman was introduced between Wolverhampton and Penzance via Honeybourne, but with the rundown of this line, it changed its route to via New Street and the Lickey Incline.

The opening of the Lifford Curve on 1 July 1892 saw the start of the circle passenger service from New Street to New Street via Camp Hill and the West Suburban lines. Trains ran mainly during peak hours and the service was withdrawn on 27 January 1941 as a wartime economy measure.

Reverting to ordinary trains, September 1937 showed a service of 11 each way and 9 on Sundays. By November 1944 there were 11 Up (7 on Sundays) and 13 Down (6 on Sundays), the fastest Down taking 1 hour 20 minutes. In 1957 there were 13 Down (15 on Saturdays and 10 on Sundays) the fastest taking 1 hour 10 minutes. 10 Up trains ran (22 on Saturdays and 10 on Sundays), the fastest taking 1 hour 14 minutes. Local passenger services were withdrawn on 4 January 1965. The timetable for 1985/86 showed 8 Down trains (7 HSTs), 10 on Saturdays (3 HSTs), and 7 on Sundays (4 HSTs). In the Up direction were 12 trains (9 HSTs), Saturdays 14 (9 HSTs) and 10 Sundays (7 HSTs). The fastest Down train took 49 minutes between Birmingham and Gloucester and the fastest Up 53 minutes.

The 2012 weekday timetable offers 20 trains between Birmingham and Gloucester; 12 Worcester to Gloucester; 26 Birmingham to Cheltenham and 61 between Cheltenham and Gloucester. In the reverse direction, 21 run between Gloucester and Birmingham; 10 between Gloucester and Worcester; 29 Cheltenham to Birmingham and 29 Gloucester to Cheltenham. On Sundays 11 run Birmingham to Gloucester; 4 Worcester to Gloucester; 20 Birmingham to Cheltenham and 16 Cheltenham to Gloucester. Up Sunday trains: 22 Gloucester to Birmingham; 4 Gloucester to Worcester; 32 Cheltenham to Birmingham and 16 Gloucester to Cheltenham.

Locomotives of the Birmingham & Gloucester Railway

No.	Name	Builder	Builder's No.	Date	Type	Notes
1	*Bromsgrove*	Forrester	-	c7/1839	2-2-2	MR No. 244. Replaced 3/1849.
2	*Tewkesbury*	Forrester	-	c9/1839	2-2-2	Sold, or used for stationary work. Not taken into MR stock.
3	*Worcester*	Forrester	-	5/1839	2-2-2	MR No.243. Replaced 2/1851.
4	*Cheltenham*	Forrester	-	c9/1839	2-2-2	Sold, or used for stationary work. Not taken into MR stock.
5	*England*	Norris	-	3/1839	4-2-0	Sold 8/1842.
6	*Victoria*	Norris	-	7/1839	4-2-0	Allotted MR No. 277 but not carried as engine was put to use for stationary work. Reinstated to traffic late 1849 or early 1850 and received its number 277. Renumbered 106 6/1852. Replaced 12/1855.
7	*Atlantic*	Norris	-	11/1839	4-2-0	Sold 7/1846 to Mr Cardis.
8	*Columbia*	Norris	-	11/1839	4-2-0	Sold 1/1846 to Aberdare Railway.
9	*Birmingham*	Norris	-	8/1840	4-2-0	Sold 4/1846 to W. Worswick.
10	*Gloucester*	Norris	-	6/1840	4-2-0	Sold 9/1845 to Taff Vale Railway.
11	*W. S. Moorsom*	Norris	-	6/1840	4-2-0	Sold 8/1845 to Taff Vale Railway.
12	*Washington*	Norris	-	8/1840	4-2-0	Sold 11/1846 to English Copper Co.
13	*Philadelphia*	Norris	-	5/1840	4-2-0	Rebuilt 3/1842 as a saddle tank. MR No. 271. Renumbered 113 6/1852. Withdrawn and broken up 6/1856.

14	*Boston*	Norris	-	8/1840	4-2-0	Rebuilt as a saddle tank by 8/1842. MR No.272. Renumbered 114 6/1852. Withdrawn and broken up 6/1856.
15	*Baltimore*	Norris	-	9/1840	4-2-0	Allotted MR No. 281 but not carried as engine was put to use for stationary work. Reinstated to traffic late 1849 or early 1850 and received its number 281. Sold 3/1852 to Mr Pickering.
16	*Moseley*	Norris	-	2/1840	4-2-0	Ex Thomas Banks, Manchester. Sold 12/1843.
17	*Pivot*	Norris	-	7/1840	4-2-0	Ex Thomas Banks, Manchester. Allotted MR No. 278 but not carried as engine was put to use for stationary work. Reinstated to traffic late 1849 or early 1850 and received its number 278. Renumbered 107 6/1852 and replaced 2/1885.
18	*Bredon*	Hick	-	10/1840	4-2-0	Allotted MR No. 279 but not carried as engine was put to use for stationary work. Reinstated to traffic late 1849 or early 1850 and received its number 279. Renumbered 108 /1852. Replaced 12/1855.
19	*Defford*	Nasmyth Gaskell	17	11/1840	4-2-0	Allotted MR No. 280 but not carried as engine was put to use for stationary work. Reinstated to traffic late 1849 or early 1850 and received its number 280. Renumbered 109 6/1852. Replaced 12/1855.
20	*President*	Norris	-	c12/1840	4-2-0	Allotted MR No. 282 but not carried as engine was put to use for stationary work. Reinstated to traffic late 1849 or early 1850 and received its number 282. Sold 3/1852 to Mr Pickering.
21	*William Gwynn*	Norris	-	2/1840	4-2-0	Rebuilt as a saddle tank by 8/1842. MR No. 273. Sold 5/1852 to Mr Knox.
22	*Leicester*	Stephenson	4	1832	0-4-0	Ex Leicester & Swannington Railway 10/1838. (Comet). Used as a ballast engine. Out of use by 8/1842 and replaced 1/1846.

23	Southampton	Jones	-	5/1837	0-4-2	Ex London & Southampton Railway 1/1839. Used as a ballast engine. Replaced 3/1846 and sold 3/1847 to Thomas Hale.
24	Spetchley	Hick	-	1841	4-2-0	Allotted MR No. 283 but never carried. Sold 3/1847 to Wykes & Porter.
25	Eckington	Hick	-	1841	4-2-0	Sold 10/1846 to B. & N. Sherwood.
26	Ashchurch	Nasmyth Gaskell	18	1/1841	4-2-0	Sold 8/1846 to George Wythes, (Brighton Railway contractor).
27	Droitwich	Nasmyth Gaskell	19	1/1841	4-2-0	Allotted MR No. 284 but never carried as engine was put to use for stationary work. Disposed of before 1849?
28	Pershore	Nasmyth Gaskell	22	6/1841	4-2-0	Sold 4/1846 to Lord Ward.
29	Upton	Nasmyth Gaskell	23	7/1841	4-2-0	Allotted MR No. 285 but never carried as engine was put to use for stationary work. Sold 3/1847 to T. Leather?
30	Lifford	Nasmyth Gaskell	24	8/1841	4-2-0	Allotted MR No. 286 but never carried as engine was put to use for stationary work. Sold 10/ 1847 to Wykes & Co?
31	Niagara	Norris	-	5/1842	4-2-0	Rebuilt as a saddle tank before 1847? MR No.274. Sold 5/1851 to C.H. Smith, Swansea?
32	New York	Norris	-	6/1842	4-2-0	Rebuilt as a saddle tank before 1847? MR No. 275. Renumbered 104 6/1852. Sold 4/1855 to John Wood, Derby.
33	Evesham	Bury	-	6/1842	2-2-0	MR No. 118. Renumbered 148 6/1852. Withdrawn 1/1854 and broken up 6/1855.
34	Kempsey	Bury	-	6/1842	2-2-0	MR No. 119. Withdrawn 6/1852 and broken up 6/1855.
35	Wadborough	Sharp	214	c2/1843	0-4-2	Purchased from builder's stock 1/1844. MR No. 296 numbered 305 6/1852. Replaced 7/1854.

36	*Bristol*	Jones & Potts	-	6/1844	0-6-0	MR No. 167. Rebuilt 10/1848. Renumbered 294 6/1852. Renumbered 222 6/1855. Broken up 6/1860.
37	*Hercules*	Jones & Potts	-	7/1844	0-6-0	MR No. 168. Renumbered 295 6/1852. Rebuilt as 0-6-0WT 4/1855. Renumbered 223 6/1855. Withdrawn 1928.
38	*Great Britain*	BGR	-	6/1845	0-6-0ST	MR No. 276. Renumbered 105 6/1852. Rebuilt as well tank 1/1853 and renumbered 300. Withdrawn 10/1861 and rebuilt as 0-6-0WT 12/1863. Renumbered 221. Withdrawn 1901. McConnell design for Lickey banking duties.

Appendix Two

Brief Details of BGR Locomotive Types

Nos.	Driving wheel diameter	Cylinders	Weight	Builder's Class
1–4	5 ft 6 in	13 in x 18 in	12 ton 10 cwt	
5, 7–12, 16 & 17	4 ft	10½ in x 18 in	10 ton 5 cwt	
6, 15 & 20	4 ft	10½ in x 18 in	11 ton 8 cwt	A
13, 14, 21, 31 & 32	4 ft	12½ in x 20 in	13 ton	A Extra
18, 24, 25	4 ft	10½ in x 18 in	11 ton 8 cwt	Hick A
19, 26–30	4 ft	10½ in x 18 in	11 tons 8 cwt	Nasmyth A
22	5 ft	12 in x 16 in	9 ton 9½ cwt	
23	5 ft	12 in x 18 in	?	
33 & 34	5 ft	13 in x 18 in	?	
35	4 ft 6 in	14 in x 20 in	?	
36 & 37	4 ft 6 in	15 in x 14 in	?	
36 Rebuilt 12/1856	5 ft	16 in x 24 in	?	
37 Rebuilt 4/1855	5 ft	16 in x 24 in	?	
38	3 ft 10 in	18 in x 26 in	30 ton	
38 Rebuilt 1/1853	3 ft 9 in	16 in x 24 in	?	

Appendix Three

Locomotives of the Bristol & Birmingham Railway

(Birmingham & Gloucester Railway and Bristol & Gloucester Railway Joint Board of Management)

No.	Name	Builder	Builder's No.	Date Built	Type	Notes
5	Camilla	Nasmyth Gaskell	9	1840	2-2-2	Purchased 12/1845 from John Hargreaves, Bolton. MR No. 104, renumbered 112 6/1852. Withdrawn 2/1854, broken up 6/1855.
10	Gloucester	Bury			0-6-0	Not taken into MR stock.
11	-	Bury			0-6-0	Not taken into MR stock.
22	Stratford	Sharp	328	1/1846	2-2-2	MR No. 53. Broken up 2/1861.
23	Atlas	Sharp	338	3/1846	2-2-2	MR No. 54. Withdrawn 7/1859, broken up 6/1860.
39	Wellington	Tayleur	-	1836	0-4-2	Purchased 12/1845 from John Hargreaves, ex-Bolton & Leigh Rly. MR No. 295. Sold to Roof & Hill 7/1849.
41	-	Tayleur	-	1846	4-2-0	MR No.88. Rebuilt c. 1849 as Jenny Lind class 2-2-2. Broken up 8/1859.
42	-	Tayleur	-	1846	4-2-0	MR No. 89. Rebuilt c. 1849 as Jenny Lind class 2-2-2. Broken up 1/1861.
43	-	Tayleur	-	1846	4-2-0	MR No.90. Rebuilt c. 1849 as Jenny Lind class 2-2-2. Withdrawn 6/1855, broken up 7/1858.
44	Vulcan	Tayleur		5/1846	0-6-0	MR No. 169. Renumbered 337 8/1862, broken up 8/1862.
45	Proserpine	Tayleur		5/1846	0-6-0	MR No. 170. Rebuilt 1/1852. Broken up 1/1863.

46	-	Tayleur	6/1846	2-4-0	MR No. 165. Renumbered 293 6/1852; 338 6/1855. Broken up 7/1858.
47	-	Tayleur	6/1846	2-4-0	MR No. 166. Renumbered 292 6/1852, 220 6/1855. Withdrawn 1/1857, broken up 7/1858.
60	*Pandora*	Tayleur	1838	0-4-2	Purchased 12/1845 from John Hargreaves, ex-Bolton & Leigh Rly. MR No.297. Renumbered 306 6/1852. Sold to Fairbanks, contractors, 7/1854.

Locomotive Builders

Birmingham & Gloucester Railway, Bromsgrove Works. Edward Bury & Co., Clarence Foundry, Love Lane, Liverpool. Geo. Forrester & Co., Vauxhall Foundry, Liverpool. Benjamin Hick, Soho Ironworks, Bolton. John Jones, Viaduct Foundry, Newton-Le-Willows. Jones & Potts, Viaduct Foundry, Newton-Le-Willows. Nasmyth Gaskell & Co., Bridgewater Foundry, Patricroft. William, Norris, Philadelphia, USA. Sharp Bros. Atlas Works, Great Bridgewater Street, Manchester. Robert Stephenson & Co., Forth Street, Newcastle-on-Tyne. Charles Tayleur & Co., Vulcan Foundry, Nr. Warrington.

Appendix Four

Statistics of the Birmingham & Gloucester Railway, 1841

Six months ending 31 December 1841.

	No. of passengers	Average number of miles travelled by each passenger
First class	50,294	24 1/5
Second class	117,660	19 1/5
Third class	25,332	19 3/5
By mail trains daily	120½	
By all other trains	946½	
By mails on Sundays	124	

Goods 1 January – 31 December 1841

	Weight (tons) by company	Weight (tons) by carriers
First quarter	4,088	3,132
Second quarter	5,881	4,043
Third quarter	2,693	2,322
Fourth quarter	3,187	1,720

Mileage of engines: 142,666 miles, coke used 2,516 tons; coke per mile 35¼ lb.

Lickey Incline 1,242 trips. Coke used 238 tons, coke per mile 438½ lb. Average number of engines in working order during six months: 23. In the first six months of 1842 these figures had been reduced to: 37¾ lbs of coke per mile; 266¾ lb per mile on the Lickey Incline.

Passenger Fares

	1840			1842			1845		
Class	1	2	3	1	2	3	1	2	3
Gloucester – Birmingham	13s 6d	9s 0d	5s 6d	14s 0d	10s 0d	5s 6d	14s 0d	10s 6d	-
Cheltenham – Birmingham	11s 6d	8s 0d	5s 0d	12s 0d	9s 0d	5s 0d	-	-	-
Cheltenham – Gloucester	2s 0d	1s 0d	0s 8d	2s 0d	1s 6d	0s 8d	-	-	-

	1840			1842			1845		
Class	1	2	3	1	2	3	1	2	3
Gloucester – London	-	-	-	36s 0d	24s 0d	-	30s 0d	20s 0d	9s 5d

Weekly Rates of Pay 1840

Engine Driver	40s (1842) (36s 1843)
Fireman	27s (1842) (23s 1843)
Guard: First class passenger	30s (20s 1842)
Second class passenger	28s (15s 1842; 25s 1845)
Third class goods	21s

Police: Road	30s
Station	18s
Station Inspector	30s (35s 1844; 30s 1845)
Porter: Train	21s
Station	18s (16s 1843; 10s 1844)
Gatekeeper	7s – 18s (1841)
Switchman	11s – 16s (1843); (18s 1844)
Ticket Collector	30s (1842); (8s – 15s 1844)
Permanent Way Overlooker	£80 per annum (£100 p.a. 1845)
Clerk: Station	21s (25s 1845)
Assistant	21s (1843)
Chief	£100 p.a. (£120 p.a. 1841; £140 p.a. 1845)
Various	£60 p.a. (£90 p.a. 1842)
Engine Driver	

Number of Staff Employed

January to June		July to December	
1841		803*	347
1842		334	313
1843		294	273

* Includes engineering department whose staff was reduced as line was completed.

Appendix Five

Locomotive Allocation, 1945

SALTLEY 21A

Stanier 3MT 2-6-2T
74, 97, 117, 175

Somerset & Dorset 2P 4-4-0
326

MR 2P 4-4-0
385, 463, 486, 493, 505, 509, 511, 512

MR 3P 4-4-0
715, 745

MR 4P 4-4-0
1015, 1029, 1035

LMS 4P 4-4-0
1055, 1064

MR 1P 0-4-4T
1338, 1367, 1411

MR 1F 0-6-0T
1682, 1777, 1856, 1879

Fowler 4MT 2-6-4T
2327

Stanier 4MT 2-6-4T
2546, 2554

5MT 2-6-0
2790, 2793, 2799, 2818, 2822, 2824, 2825,
2826, 2829, 2900, 2903

MR 2F 0-6-0
2994, 3085, 3103, 3110, 3138, 3311, 3432,
3473, 3516, 3527, 3535, 3592, 3699, 3758,
22946, 22947, 22953, 22955

MR 3F 0-6-0
3201, 3203, 3223, 3225, 3277, 3284, 3321, 3336,
3339, 3359, 3374, 3433, 3435, 3441, 3443, 3484,
3490, 3491, 3522, 3523, 3529, 3531, 3540, 3568,
3621, 3624, 3644, ,3667, 3674, 3680, 3684,
3686, 3690, 3698, 3767, 3812

MR 4F 0-6-0
3845, 3879, 3911, 3912, 3940, 3941, 3949,
3951, 3986

LMS 4F 0-6-0
4049, 4084, 4088, 4092, 4137, 4139, 4145,
4184, 4185, 4186, 4190, 4200, 4203, 4207,
4213, 4224, 4248, 4304, 4327, 4333, 4406,
4413, 4427, 4515, 4516, 4520, 4524, 4525,
4538, 4545, 4567, 4591

5MT 4-6-0
4811, 4813, 4814, 4840, 4841, 4842, 4852,
5186, 5265, 5268, 5269, 5273, 5274, 5447

5XP 4-6-0
5641 *Sandwich*, 5709 *Implacable*

MR 3F 0-6-0T
7239, 7249

LMS 3F 0-6-0T
7273, 7276, 7425, 7436, 7443, 7638, 7639

8F 2-8-0
8351, 8389, 8669

7F 0-8-0
9672, 9673, 9674

MR double-framed 2F 0-6-0
22846

Total: 168 locomotives.

BOURNVILLE 21B

Stanier 3MT 2-6-2T
105, 173, 179

MR 2P 4-4-0
439, 517

LMS 4P 4-4-0
917, 934, 1073, 1077

MR 1F 0-6-0T
1699

Fowler 4MT 2-6-4T
2337, 2342, 2373

Standier 4MT 2-6-4T
2559

MR 3F 0-6-0
3316, 3355, 3463, 3562, 3675, 3687

LMS 4F 0-6-0
4138, 4289

MR double-framed 2F 0-6-0
22579, 22630, 22818, 22834, 22853, 22863

Total: 28 locomotives.

BROMSGROVE 21C

0-10-0
2290

MR 2F 0-6-0
3099, 3150

MR 3F 0-6-0T
7234

LMS 3F 0-6-0T
7301, 7303, 7305, 7308, 7313, 7365

Total: 10 locomotives.

GLOUCESTER 22B

MR 2P 4-4-0
423, 437, 523, 530

MR 4P 4-4-0
1001, 1027, 1036

LMS 4P 4-4-0
1097

MR 1P 0-4-4T
1303, 1330, 1353, 1365, 1375, 1390

MR 0F 0-4-0T
1530, 1537
MR 1F 0-6-0T
1720, 1742, 1870, 1878

5MT 2-6-0
2812

MR 2F 0-6-0
3062, 3695

MR3F 0-6-0
3213, 3527, 3258, 3263, 3273, 3344, 3373,
3427, 3462, 3506, 3507, 3604, 3645, 3658,
3754, 3788, 3791

MR 4F 0-6-0
3846, 3924, 3932, 3935, 3964, 3978

LMS 4F 0-6-0
4045, 4167, 4175, 4269, 4279, 4553, 4576

MR 3F 0-6-0T
7237

LMS 3F 0-6-0T
7619, 7620, 7635

Total: 57 locomotives.

Bibliography

Ahrons, E. L., *Locomotive & Train Working in the Latter Part of the Nineteenth Century* (Cambridge: Heffer, 1953)

Allen, C. J., *Titled Trains of the Western* (Shepperton: Ian Allan, 1974)

Barnes, E. G., *The Rise of the Midland Railway 1844–1874* (London: Allen & Unwin, 1966)

Baxter, B., *British Locomotive Catalogue 1825–1923. Vol. 3A* (Ashbourne: Moorland, 1982)

Bick, D. E., *The Gloucester & Cheltenham Tramroad* (Headington: Oakwood Press, 1987)

Biddle, G., *The Railway Surveyors* (Shepperton: Ian Allan, 1990)

Birmingham & Gloucester Railway Minute Books, Public Record Office RAIL 37.1; RAIL 37.27

Binney, M. & Pearce, D., *Railway Architecture* (London: Bloomsbury Books, 1985)

Boynton, J., *Rails Across The City* (Kidderminster: Mid England Books, 1993)

Brooksbank, B. W. L., *Railway Damage and Disruption in World War II* (Backtrack, September 2004)

Brown, P. A., *Many and Great Inconveniences,* Swindon (South Western Circle, 2003)

Casserley, H. C., *The Lickey Incline* (Headington: Oakwood Press, 1990)

Christiansen, R., *Regional History of Railways of Great Britain, Volume 13 Thames & Severn* (Newton Abbot: David & Charles, 1981)

Clinker, C. R., *Railways of the West Midlands, A Chronology 1808–1954* (Stephenson Locomotive Society)

Clinker, C. R., *Closed Stations & Goods Depots* (Weston-super-Mare: Avon-Anglia, 1988)

Collins, P., *Britain's Rail Super Centres: Birmingham* (Shepperton: Ian Allan, 1992)

Cooke, R. A., *Track Layout Diagrams of the GWR & BR WR. Sections 34 & 35* (Didcot: R. A. Cooke, 1977)

Dewhurst, P. C., *Norris Locomotives In England,* Newcomen Society Transactions Volume XXVI (1947–49)

Dixon, J., (compiler), *19th Century British Railway Accidents* (Chester: J. Dixon, 1991)

Ellis, G. H., *The Midland Railway* (Shepperton: Ian Allan, 1966)

Essery, R. J. & Jenkinson, D., *An Illustrated Review Of Midland Locomotives* (Didcot: Wild Swan, 1988)

Hawkins, C. & Reeves., G, *LMS Engine Sheds, Volume 2* (Didcot: Wild Swan, 1981)

Hewison, C. H., *Locomotive Boiler Explosions* (Newton Abbot: David & Charles, 1983)

Hitches, M., *Worcestershire Railways* (Stroud: Sutton Publishing, 1997)

Long, P. J. & Awdry, Revd W. V., *The Birmingham and Gloucester Railway* (Gloucester: Alan Sutton, 1987)

MacDermot, E. T., revised Clinker, C. R., *History of the Great Western Railway* (Shepperton: Ian Allan, 1964)

Midland Railway System Maps Volume 4, The Distance Diagrams Birmingham to Bristol (Teignmouth, Peter Kay)

Midland Railway System Maps Volume 6 The Gradient Diagrams (Teignmouth: Peter Kay)

Maggs, C. G., *The Bristol & Gloucester Railway* (Headington: Oakwood Press, 1992; 3rd edn, Stroud: Amberley Publishing, 2013)

Mitchell, V., & Smith, K., *Bromsgrove to Birmingham* (Midhurst: Middleton Press, 2006)
Mitchell, V., & Smith, K., *Bromsgrove to Gloucester* (Midhurst: Middleton Press, 2006)
Mourton, S., *Steam Routes Around Cheltenham* (Cheltenham: Runpast Publishing, 1993)
Oakely, M., *Gloucestershire Railway Stations* (Dovecote Press, 2003)
Perkins, T. R., *The Lickey Incline*, Railway Magazine (October 1904)
Rake, H., *The South Western Extension of the Midland Railway* (Railway Magazine, February 1904)
Reed, B., *Loco Profile No.11 The Norris Locomotives* (Profile Publications Ltd, 1971)
Signalling Record Society Newsletter, Nos. 62, 65
Simmons, J., *The Railways of Britain* (London: Routledge & Kegan Paul, 1962)
Smith, D. J. M. & Harrison, D., *Over The Lickey* (Woodchester: Peter Watts Publishing, 1990)
Spencer, H., *An Autobiography* (London: Williams & Norgate, 1904)
Williams, F. S., *The Midland Railway* (Newton Abbot: David & Charles, 1968)

Index